access to history

THE UNIFICATION OF GERMANY 1815–90

Second Edition

access to history

THE UNIFICATION OF GERMANY 1815–90

Second Edition

Andrina Stiles and Alan Farmer

Hodder & Stoughton

A MEMBER OF THE HODDER HEADLINE GROUP

Acknowledgements

The front cover illustration shows a portrait of Otto von Bismarck, Mansell/Timepix/ Rex Features.

The publishers would like to thank the following individuals, institutions and companies for permission to reproduce copyright illustrations in this book: AKG Photo London, page 56; Napoleon III. und Bismarck am Morgen nach der Schlacht bei Sedan by Wilhelm Camphausen, AKG Photo, page 89; © Bettmann/CORBIS, page 14; Bildarchiv Preubischer Kulturbesitz. Geschichte Deutschland 19th Revolution 1848, Karikaturen zur Europaischen Lage 'Rundgemalde von Europe im August 1848', page 48; Proclamation of Kaiser Wilhelmm, 1871 by Anton Alexander von Werner, Schloss Friedrichsruhe, Germany/Bridgeman Art Library, page 93; Punch, page 130.

The publishers would also like to thank the following for permission to reproduce material in this book:

HarperCollins for the extract from *The Fontana History of Germany 1780–1918: The Long Nineteenth Century* by David Blackbourn (Fontana, 1997); Pearson Education Ltd for the extract from *Bismarck, Kaiser and Germany* by Elliot (Longman).

Every effort has been made to trace and acknowledge ownership of copyright. The publishers will be glad to make suitable arrangements with any copyright holders whom it has not been possible to contact.

Orders: please contact Bookpoint Ltd, 130 Milton Park, Abingdon, Oxon OX14 4SB. Telephone: (44) 01235 827720, Fax: (44) 01235 400454. Lines are open from 9.00–6.00, Monday to Saturday, with a 24 hour message answering service. You can also order through our website at www.hodderline.co.uk

British Library Cataloguing in Publication Data
A catalogue record for this title is available from the British Library

ISBN 0 340 78142 4

First published 2001
Impression number   10 9 8 7 6 5
Year   2007 2006 2005 2004

Copyright © 2001 Andrina Stiles and Alan Farmer

Typeset by Fakenham Photosetting Ltd, Fakenham, Norfolk.
Printed in Great Britain for Hodder & Stoughton Educational, 338 Euston Road, London NW1 3BH by CPI Bath

Contents

Preface

To the general reader

Although the *Access to History* series has been designed with the needs of students studying the subject at higher examination levels very much in mind, it also has a great deal to offer the general reader. The main body of the text (i.e. ignoring the 'Study Guides' at the ends of chapters) forms a readable and yet stimulating survey of a coherent topic as studied by historians. However, each author's aim has not merely been to provide a clear explanation of what happened in the past (to interest and inform): it has also been assumed that most readers wish to be stimulated into thinking further about the topic and to form opinions of their own about the significance of the events that are described and discussed (to be challenged). Thus, although no prior knowledge of the topic is expected on the reader's part, she or he is treated as an intelligent and thinking person throughout. The author tends to share ideas and possibilities with the reader, rather than passing on numbers of so-called 'historical truths'.

To the student reader

Although advantage has been taken of the publication of a second edition to ensure the results of recent research are reflected in the text, the main alteration from the first edition is the inclusion of new features, and the modification of existing ones, aimed at assisting you in your study of the topic at AS level, A level and Higher. Two features are designed to assist you during your first reading of a chapter. The *Points to Consider* section following each chapter title is intended to focus your attention on the main theme(s) of the chapter, and the issues box following most section headings alerts you to the question or questions to be dealt with in the section. The *Working on...* section at the end of each chapter suggests ways of gaining maximum benefit from the chapter.

There are many ways in which the series can be used by students studying History at a higher level. It will, therefore, be worthwhile thinking about your own study strategy before you start your work on this book. Obviously, your strategy will vary depending on the aim you have in mind, and the time for study that is available to you.

If, for example, you want to acquire a general overview of the topic in the shortest possible time, the following approach will probably be the most effective:

1. Read chapter 1. As you do so, keep in mind the issues raised in the *Points to Consider* section.
2. Read the *Points to Consider* section at the beginning of chapter 2 and decide whether it is necessary for you to read this chapter.
3. If it is, read the chapter, stopping at each heading or sub-heading to note

down the main points that have been made. Often, the best way of doing this is to answer the question(s) posed in the Key Issues boxes.

4. Repeat stage 2 (and stage 3 where appropriate) for all the other chapters.

If, however, your aim is to gain a thorough grasp of the topic, taking however much time is necessary to do so, you may benefit from carrying out the same procedure with each chapter, as follows:

1. Try to read the chapter in one sitting. As you do this, bear in mind any advice given in the *Points to Consider* section.
2. Study the flow diagram at the end of the chapter, ensuring that you understand the general 'shape' of what you have just read.
3. Read the *Working on...* section and decide what further work you need to do on the chapter. In particularly important sections of the book, this is likely to involve reading the chapter a second time and stopping at each heading and sub-heading to think about (and probably to write a summary of) what you have just read.
4. Attempt the *Source-based questions* section. It will sometimes be sufficient to think through your answers, but additional understanding will often be gained by forcing yourself to write them down.

When you have finished the main chapters of the book, study the 'Further Reading' section and decide what additional reading (if any) you will do on the topic.

This book has been designed to help make your studies both enjoyable and successful. If you can think of ways in which this could have been done more effectively, please contact us. In the meantime, we hope that you will gain greatly from your study of History.

Keith Randell & Robert Pearce

Introduction: The Unification of Germany, 1815–90

POINTS TO CONSIDER

In January 1871 King William I of Prussia became Kaiser (or Emperor) of the new German Empire. The creation of the Empire was one of the most important developments of the nineteenth century. The process by which Germany came to be unified has been an area of historical debate ever since. This short introductory chapter is designed to do no more than set the scene. It aims to introduce you to themes that will be explored in more depth later in the book.

Before 1871 Germany did not exist as a country in the sense of being a unified political state. Throughout the Middle Ages and the early modern period, indeed right up to the early nineteenth century, the area generally known as Germany was made up of hundreds of separate states. These ranged from small city states and small areas of countryside ruled over by noblemen to large and powerful kingdoms, such as Prussia. All belonged to the Holy Roman Empire. (According to the French philosopher Voltaire, it was neither Holy, Roman nor an Empire.) The Holy Roman Emperor, who was in nominal control over the archaic Empire, had little power, apart from that gained by having territories to rule over in his own right.

To make the situation more complicated, Germany lacked clear natural frontiers, especially in the east and in the south. It was not even possible to define its extent on ethnic grounds. In many areas the population was a mixture of German and Slav speakers such as Poles and Czechs, while some regions peopled almost entirely by Germans were cut off from their fellow German speakers by large communities of other ethnic groups. It did not even make sense to work by the boundaries of the Holy Roman Empire because these included much land peopled by French, Dutch, Danish, Polish and Czech speakers and excluded sizeable territories with a predominantly German population.

Each Holy Roman Emperor was elected to his position. It was therefore possible in theory for any family to supply an emperor, but in practice only members of the Habsburg family were chosen. They ruled extensive territories which centred on Austria. The Habsburg Empire – known as Austria or the Austrian Empire between 1815 and 1867, and as Austria-Hungary or the Dual Monarchy between 1867 and 1918 – included much of the southern part of what was known as Germany. The Habsburgs were Germans and their empire had been regarded as the leading German power for many years before 1815.

In 1815 two German states were to be numbered among the five European Great Powers. The first (and stronger of the two) was Austria. The other (and the least important of the Great Powers) was Prussia. By a series of annexations and marriages with heiresses Prussia had grown from relative insignificance to major power status in a little more than a century. Like Austria, she had suffered badly at the hands of Napoleon but she had recovered and her armies had played a large part in the eventual defeat of the French after 1813.

Although it was not recognised at the time, the seeds were sown for a shift in the balance between the two German Powers in the Vienna Settlement of 1815, which distributed territory at the end of the Napoleonic Wars. Whereas Austria acquired new possessions outside Germany (mainly in Italy), Prussia gained extensively in western Germany, lost Polish lands to Russia, and in the process turned herself from being a state with interests mainly in eastern Germany to being the dominant power in the whole of the northern half of Germany. The events discussed in this book are mainly concerned with how this situation developed to produce the unitary political state of Germany.

The struggle between Austria and Prussia for mastery in Germany is not, however, the only theme that needs to be explored. There were many Germans at the time who did not see matters in terms of power politics. Even in 1815 there were tens of thousands of people, especially among the young, the educated, and the middle and upper classes, who felt passionately that Germans deserved to have a fatherland in the same way as the English and French already had. They longed for a united Germany to give visible form to their strongly-held sense of national identity. The numbers of these German nationalists grew greatly in the years after 1815. They came near to achieving their objective in 1848, but they failed. How and why they failed needs to be investigated.

Many of the early successes in bringing about a more united Germany were achieved in economic affairs rather than in the field of politics. It is important to understand what these were and to consider what part they played in shaping the form that unification eventually took.

Historians differ in their views on the relative importance of impersonal forces, such as economics, and the work of individuals in bringing about major changes in the past. The latter stages of German unification were dominated by one man, Otto von Bismarck. Some would argue that he masterminded the whole affair; others would say that he unscrupulously manipulated situations as they arose to gain an advantage for his state, Prussia. Others again would maintain that his actions were largely irrelevant because greater forces, especially of ideas and economics, were at work that would have ensured eventual unification whatever Bismarck or other politicians had done. The evidence allows each of these interpretations to be supported and we are left searching for the balance of probability.

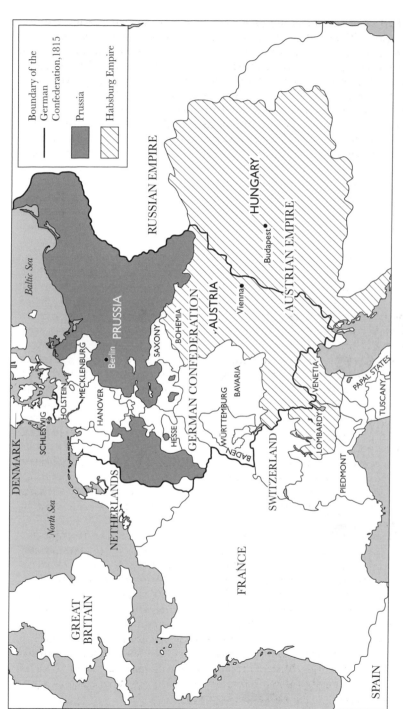

Germany in 1815

The state of Germany came into existence in 1871. But although the new country was united in that it could be coloured the same shade on the map, in many important respects there was no unity. In the next 20 years Bismarck tried to extend the existing political unification. The problems he faced need to be understood and an assessment made of how far he was successful in solving them.

Thus several major issues need to be kept in mind as this book is read. Some are themes that appear throughout; others are restricted to particular sections. The flow diagram on page 5 provides a summary of some of the main events that you are about to explore.

Summary Diagram
The Unification of Germany, 1815–90

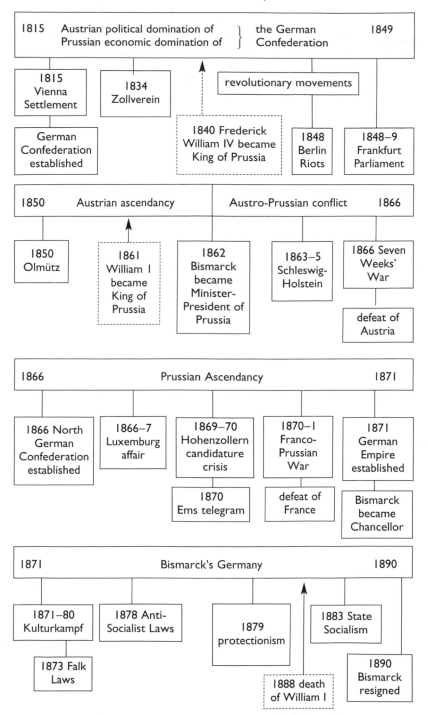

1815	Austrian political domination of the German	1849
	Prussian economic domination of } Confederation	

1815 Vienna Settlement

1834 Zollverein

revolutionary movements

German Confederation established

1840 Frederick William IV became King of Prussia

1848 Berlin Riots

1848–9 Frankfurt Parliament

1850	Austrian ascendancy	Austro-Prussian conflict	1866

1850 Olmütz

1861 William I became King of Prussia

1862 Bismarck became Minister-President of Prussia

1863–5 Schleswig-Holstein

1866 Seven Weeks' War

defeat of Austria

1866	Prussian Ascendancy	1871

1866 North German Confederation established

1866–7 Luxemburg affair

1869–70 Hohenzollern candidature crisis

1870 Ems telegram

1870–1 Franco-Prussian War

defeat of France

1871 German Empire established

Bismarck became Chancellor

1871	Bismarck's Germany	1890

1871–80 Kulturkampf

1878 Anti-Socialist Laws

1879 protectionism

1883 State Socialism

1873 Falk Laws

1888 death of William I

1890 Bismarck resigned

1 Germany 1815–48

POINTS TO CONSIDER

The years 1815–1848 are often called the *Vormärz* or pre-March (a prelude to the March revolution in Berlin in 1848). Associated with the Austrian statesman Metternich, the *Vormärz* is usually seen as a period of illiberality and repression. Is this fair? To what extent did the period see the development of liberalism and nationalism in Germany? We also have to ask how united Germany was by 1848.

KEY DATES

1813 Battle of Leipzig.
1815 German Confederation established.
1817 Wartburg Festival.
1819 Carlsbad Decrees.
1832 Nationalist festival at Hambach.
1834 Zollverein came into operation.
1840 Frederick William IV became King of Prussia.
1847 Meeting of the Prussian United Diet in Berlin.

1 The German Confederation

> **KEY ISSUE** How united was Germany in 1815?

a) German Disunity

The term 'Germany' had no real political significance before the nineteenth century. There was no single German state. At the end of the eighteenth century some 23 million Germans were divided into 314 states, varying in size from the 115,533 square miles of the Habsburg monarchy to the 33 square miles of Schwartzburg-Sonderhausen. These states were loosely united under the nominal rule of the Holy Roman Emperor, who was also Emperor of Austria. Apart from Austria, only one state within the Empire had any real power or importance, and that was Prussia. When first Austria in 1805 and then Prussia in 1806 were defeated by Napoleon I, the Holy Roman Empire collapsed.

Napoleon reorganised the old hotchpotch of states. France annexed the territory on the left bank of the Rhine. Elsewhere many small states were amalgamated and the total number was reduced to 39. Bavaria, Saxony, Baden and 14 other states were formed into the Confederation of the Rhine. This Confederation was under direct French control, and the French legal system replaced the different laws and judicial procedures of the separate states. A small beginning had been made in the political and judicial unification of Germany. The French Revolution and Napoleonic conquests transformed the German political landscape in other ways. Revolutionary ideas of liberty, equality and fraternity created a new context for German politics. There was increased middle-class involvement in government and in administration. Large numbers of Germans were released from feudal restrictions for the first time.

After the devastating defeat by Napoleon in 1806 and the humiliating loss of a large part of her territory, Prussia was determined to recover her position as a leading German state by driving out the French. Impressed by French military successes, the Prussian government decided to copy what had been done in revolutionary France. Under the leadership of Baron Stein, Hardenberg, Scharnhorst and Gneisenau, efforts were made to reform Prussian institutions. Prussian serfs were emancipated. The rigid class system was relaxed. The army was reorganised and rebuilt to a high standard of military preparedness. The government was overhauled and modernised to provide a strong and efficient central authority. A new system of education was introduced to encourage Prussian patriotic feeling among students. Popular anti-French opinion encouraged King Frederick William III to overcome his natural indecisiveness and in January 1813 he made an alliance with Russia against France. The Russian and Prussian armies launched a campaign to drive Napoleon's forces back towards France. In June Austria also declared war on France and in October Napoleon was defeated at the Battle of Leipzig. The French lost 50,000 men and were forced back to the River Rhine. Within a few months the allied armies invaded France and forced Napoleon to abdicate. The so-called War of Liberation has often been seen as the first collective action of the German nation. However, later nationalist myths of the War of Liberation bore little relation to reality. German resistance to France never became a mass national uprising. South Germans tended to look to Austria for political leadership; North Germans tended to look to Prussia. It was clear from the start that the future of Germany would be decided, not by German patriots but by the particular interests of Prussia and Austria.

b) The Vienna Settlement

In 1814–5 German unification was not a practical proposition. Too many deep-seated divisions stood in the way of national unity. Perhaps the most important was the rivalry between Austria and Prussia. Dominating the remaining states, these two powerful states were obvious rival candidates for the control of any united Germany. However, at this stage, they were content to exist side by side in what Austrian

Foreign Minister Metternich called 'peaceful dualism'. Both were among the Great Powers who drew up the peace treaty at the Congress of Vienna in 1815. Not surprisingly, both benefited substantially from the Vienna settlement.

Prussia gained considerable areas of territory, including part of Saxony and the valuable Rhineland, as well as Westphalia and Pomerania. This more than compensated for the loss of much of her Polish territory to Russia and meant that the population of the Kingdom of Prussia had been more than doubled to ten million. The Vienna Settlement ensured that Prussia was the dominant power in northern Germany.

The sudden increase in size brought problems, particularly with the Rhineland. There most of the population were Catholics, while nearly all Prussians were Protestant. The Rhinelanders resented being annexed to Prussia from which they were separated by more than 80 kilometres and with which they had little in common. Not only were there differences in religion but in customs and traditions as well. The industrialised Rhineland with its numerous towns contrasted sharply with rural Prussia. It had come under French influence as part of Napoleon's Confederation of the Rhine, and Rhinelanders considered themselves part of western Europe. Many regarded the Prussians as an alien culture from the east.

Prussia had done as much if not more than Austria in driving the French out of Germany, but was able to exercise less influence at the Peace Congress. This was mainly because the Prussian delegation was handicapped in negotiations by the inconsistent policies of the Prussian King and his refusal to follow his ministers' advice. The most important influence on the future of the German states was that of Metternich. His aim was the maintenance of Austria's traditional authority over the German states. He was not concerned with German political unity, and his negotiations ensured that Germany would become a loose confederation of states under Austrian control.

In June 1815 the German Confederation was established. The Confederation had 39 states, far less than the hundreds of states that had existed in the late eighteenth century. The Napoleonic reorganisation of Germany was thus, in part, allowed to stand. The Great Powers turned a deaf ear to the claims of most of the princes who asked for the restoration of their tiny principalities. The Confederation's declared aim was to ensure 'the external and internal security and the independence and integrity of the individual states'. In essence this meant the maintenance of the status quo in individual states through a system of mutual assistance in times of danger, such as internal rebellion or external aggression (especially from France). It was not interested in or concerned with promoting a united Germany. In fact its aim was exactly the opposite, for the rulers of the separate states did not wish to see their independence limited by the establishment of a power organisation covering the whole of Germany. Thus no objection was raised when the boundaries of the Confederation were modelled on those of the old Holy Roman Empire rather than on ones that would encourage the development of a nation state of Germany. So areas peopled by Poles, Czechs, Danes and French were included and provinces with largely German-speaking populations were excluded. States such as Luxemburg, Hanover and Holstein which were ruled over by foreign monarchs (the Dutch King ruled Luxemburg, the British King Hanover and the Danish King Holstein) were within the Confederation while large parts of German-speaking Austria and Prussia were not.

c) The Diet

The Confederation had only one executive body, the *Bundestag* or Diet, which met at Frankfurt. This was a permanent conference of – essentially – ambassadors who were not elected but were sent by their governments with instructions how to act, and was presided over by the Austrian representative. The Diet met for the first time at the end of 1816. It was soon clear that little would be achieved. For one thing the agreement of every state government was required before any measure could be passed. This total agreement was seldom forthcoming, for representatives were more concerned with safeguarding the interests and sovereignty of their states than working for the Confederation as a whole.

Each German state had its own independent ruler, its own government and its own army. The Confederation appointed ambassadors and could make foreign treaties on behalf of its members. Otherwise it had very little direct control over the individual states, apart from being able to prevent them making foreign alliances which might threaten the security of the Confederation, or concluding separate peace agreements in the event of the Confederation being involved in war. The Constitution of the Confederation, the Federal Act, had empowered the Diet to organise a Federal Army and to develop commercial and economic co-operation between the states, but local jealousies and fiercely guarded independence meant that nothing of importance was done to unify the Confederation militarily or economically. The defence of the Confederation depended upon the continued co-operation of Austria and Prussia.

The Confederation thus disappointed those Germans who hoped for greater national unity. It has also been criticised by historians who see it as essentially the Holy Roman Empire mark two – an organisation which had no place in the age of emergent nation states. It certainly failed to create genuinely 'national' institutions. However, the

Confederation at least provided a framework within which German states co-existed, albeit uneasily. It can thus be seen as a step forward on the road to nationhood.

d) The Restoration of Monarchical Rule

Absolute, monarchical rule was restored in most German states in 1815. All but four were dynastic states – monarchies, duchies and principalities. However, one of the most important Articles of the Federal Act had laid down that the ruler of each state should sooner or later give his subjects a 'Constitution of Regional Estates'. The response varied. Some rulers totally ignored the Article. However, most of the small north German states, and some of the larger ones such as Hanover and Saxony, allowed the 'estates' to meet. These 'estates' were traditional representative bodies, not always elected, and usually composed largely of nobles. In southern and central Germany there was even more compliance with the Federal Act. In the years between 1818 and 1820 Bavaria, Baden, Württemberg and Hesse-Darmstadt introduced constitutions modelled on the French Charter of 1814. Elected assemblies were created which had the power to make laws and control taxation. However, even in these states the assemblies had limited influence. The monarchs continued to appoint their own ministers and retain real power.

Developments in Austria and Prussia were vital. Little was done to encourage democratic reform in Austria. Austrian Kings Francis I (1804–35) and his weak-minded successor Ferdinand I (1835–49) wished to maintain their absolute power. The old provincial diets were eventually revived but only as a means of preserving the existing social order. They were dominated by the local aristocracy. In Prussia Frederick William III showed little interest in liberal reform. However, in 1823 he did agree to set up provincial estates with limited advisory powers. These were completely dominated by large landowners. Following the lead of Austria and Prussia, the majority of German rulers clung obstinately to their virtually absolute power.

Noble families continued to wield huge power, dominating the political, administrative and military institutions of most German states. Interestingly, many states emerged from the years of war with better organised and more powerful bureaucracies. This was the result of either French occupation, imitation of French methods, or simply financial necessity. The bureaucracies were active in a host of areas – social, economic, legal and educational. They ensured, for example, that educational provision in Germany was the best in Europe.

2 Political Movements Working for Reform

> **KEY ISSUE** To what extent did nationalist and liberal ideas
> develop in the period 1815–48?

Student societies with a strong political flavour had grown up in the universities in 1813 after the battle of Leipzig, which drove the French out of the German states. The defeat of Napoleon was a great encouragement to German nationalism. In the years after 1815 thousands of young middle- and upper-class Germans longed for a united Germany to give visible form to their strongly held, romantic sense of national identity. Students joined *Burscherschaften* societies which campaigned for a united Germany while the growing 'gymnasium' movement instructed young men in physical activities and the national spirit. In 1817 nationalist students converted the Wartburg Festival from a celebration of the tercentenary of Martin Luther's stand against the Pope and the fourth anniversary of the victory of Leipzig into a demonstration against the princes. Given that fewer that 500 students attended the Festival, its importance has often been exaggerated.

Metternich certainly exaggerated the importance of the student movements, especially when in 1819 a member of an extreme student society murdered Kotzebue, a reactionary writer and a secret agent of the Russian Tsar. This murder prompted Metternich to take action. He consulted the King of Prussia (who agreed with Metternich on the need for stern measures) and then summoned representatives of the German states to meet him at Carlsbad. Their decisions were ratified – unanimously – by the Diet as the Carlsbad Decrees. These provided inspectors for universities, while student societies were disbanded, press censorship introduced and a commission set up to investigate so-called revolutionary movements. As a result of the Decrees a number of professors were dismissed from their posts and a few radical leaders were imprisoned. It seemed that reactionary forces had triumphed. In 1820 Metternich, suspicious of even the limited constitutions of the south German states, sought their abolition at the Congress of Troppau. He failed, but in 1821 he made it more difficult for liberal ideas to gain ground by persuading all the states to restrict the subjects which their assemblies could discuss.

The liberal ideas which Metternich so distrusted were concerned with constitutional reform and the replacing of an absolute and autocratic government by a parliamentary system firmly based on the rule of law. Liberals spoke of human rights and freedoms – freedom of speech, freedom of the press, freedom of worship, freedom to form political associations and freedom to hold political meetings. Their ideas on parliamentary representation were restricted to giving the vote to men of property. There was no question of a universal franchise, for liberals were almost exclusively well-educated, well-to-do members of the middle class concerned with their own economic and political interests and not with radical changes in the structure of society. Liberals were generally opposed to violence and hoped to achieve their aims by intellectual argument and peaceful persuasion. Too often though, talk became a substitute for action.

Many liberals were also nationalists, but not all nationalists were liberals. Some nationalists were conservatives: others held revolutionary political views. In the late eighteenth century, nationalism (the belief in a national identity) became merged with the idea of an independent state with fixed geographical boundaries and its own government. The national identity could be based on some or all the elements of a common race, language, culture, religion or geographical area. In some countries where all or most of these elements were present, strong nationalist movements developed quickly and successfully. In Germany there was no religious unity; the south and west were mainly Catholic and the north Lutheran Protestant. There were no clearly defined frontiers either. But there was a common language and a shared cultural tradition based on a literary and artistic heritage. In addition there was felt to be a racial bond uniting all Germans, and this was to become more important over the years.

The seeds of German nationalism had been sown by the philosopher Herder in the late eighteenth century. He had taught that all people or races had their own unique spirit. People living in different areas of the world developed in different ways and produced their own culture, tradition, customs and way of life. These cultures should be cherished and developed as the basis for a national identity. Herder's ideas of a cultural basis for nationhood were taken up and expanded by others, the most important of whom was Hegel, a professor in the University of Berlin. He taught that man only achieved his full potential as a human being by service to the state. As an individual he was nothing, as part of a national community he was everything.

For many ordinary Germans, German nationalism arose simply as a resentment of French rule. Once French occupation had ended, nationalist sentiment declined. The well-educated middle classes, many of whom believed that German culture – literature, music, art and philosophy – was pre-eminent in Europe, tended to have more positive views about nationalism. But only a small minority envisaged a strong united German nation which would dominate Europe.

The *Vormärz* years were certainly a time of political excitement. But much of it was of an intellectual and theoretical kind. Lectures, debates, books and pamphlets, which put forward the new ideas of liberalism and nationalism, reached only a limited audience, rarely filtering down from the educated minority to the rest of the population.

In some cases, however, the liberal-nationalist message was carried to the workers in the cities by well-meaning liberals who set up study groups, and groups were sometimes formed by workers themselves. Some groups had several hundred members, like those in Hamburg, and they discussed politics and planned revolution, or at least strike action. Their politics became democratic rather than liberal, centred on the sovereignty of the people rather than on the sovereignty of parliament, on a republic rather than a monarchy, and on violence rather than on peaceful means to obtain their ends. But however enthusiastic these groups were, they involved only a small proportion of workers in the cities and the workers on the land hardly at all. Liberalism and nationalism remained largely middle-class before 1848.

3 Repression

> **KEY ISSUE** How successful were Metternich's repressive policies?

a) Metternich

The development of liberalism and nationalism made Metternich extremely uneasy about the future of the German Confederation. If allowed to go unchecked, they could only lead to the overthrow of absolute governments in the individual states and to demands for a united Germany, with national and state representative assemblies. These demands might be at the moment only the noisy clamour of a few 'intellectuals' and workers, but the danger was that they could become the basis of popular revolution which could lead to the overthrow of absolute monarchy and the end of the multi-national Austrian Empire. Metternich believed that the maintenance of international peace was directly linked with the prevention of revolution in individual states. Internal and international affairs were inseparable. What happened inside one state was of concern to other states, and entitled them to intervene if they considered it necessary. The social order had to be defended against the forces of destruction – which Metternich saw as nationalism and liberalism. He therefore set his face against any constitutional change, however modest.

b) The Congress of Troppau

The Vienna Settlement had restored many of the monarchs of Europe to their thrones and Metternich was determined that they

METTERNICH

1773 born into high German nobility in the Rhineland
1794 his family moved to Vienna to escape a French invasion of the Rhineland
1809 became Foreign Minister of Austria
1814–5 played a key role at the Vienna Peace Settlement
1821 became Austrian Chancellor
1848 forced to resign and flee to England
1859 died.

Metternich was a complex personality. Vain, arrogant, pompous and frivolous, he was also extremely able. He saw little point in false modesty. In 1819 he said:

> There is a wide sweep about my mind. I am always above and beyond the preoccupations of most public men; I cover a ground much vaster than they can see or wish to see. I cannot keep myself from saying about twenty times a day: 'O Lord! how right I am and
> 5 how wrong they are.'

Although confident in his own abilities and ideals, he was pessimistic about the future.

> My life has coincided with a most abominable time ... I have come into the world too soon or too late. I know that in these years I can accomplish nothing ... I am spending my life underpinning buildings which are mouldering into decay.

Metternich's foreign and domestic policies seem to demonstrate a large degree of common purpose: to prevent revolution and to preserve rule by monarchy and the social dominance of the aristocracy. He believed that popular challenges to legitimate authority would result in chaos, bloodshed and an end to civilisation. His single-mindedness prompted contemporaries to speak of a 'Metternich System' and historians have subsequently found this a useful concept to help analyse his actions. Some think his 'System' was based on a complex philosophy. Others, like A.J.P. Taylor, have doubted whether there was a 'System', believing that Metternich was simply a traditional (but very able) conservative with no profound philosophical beliefs: his main aims were simply to maintain the Austrian Empire and maintain himself in office.

should be kept there. He developed the idea of European Congresses, meetings of the Great Powers to discuss and settle international disagreements and maintain peace. Four such Congresses were held between 1818 and 1822 and at one of them, the Congress of Troppau in 1820, discussion centred on the revolutions which had broken out in Spain, Portugal and Naples. All of these states had demanded constitutions from their rulers. During the Congress, Metternich sent a secret memorandum to the Tsar of Russia:

1 Kings have to calculate the chances of their very existence in the immediate future; passions are let loose, and league together to overthrow everything which society respects as the basis of its existence; religion, public morality, laws, customs, rights, and duties, all are
5 attacked, confounded, overthrown, or called into question. The great mass of the people are tranquil spectators of these attacks and revolutions ... A few are carried off by the torrent, but the wishes of the immense majority are to maintain a repose which exists no longer ...
10 There is besides scarcely any epoch which does not offer a rallying cry to some particular faction. This cry, since 1815, has been Constitution. But do not let us deceive ourselves: this word, susceptible of great latitude of interpretation, would be but imperfectly understood if we supposed that the factions attached quite the
15 same meaning to it under the different regimes. Such is certainly not the case. In pure monarchies it is qualified by the name of 'national representation'. In countries which have lately been brought under the representative regime it is called 'development', and promises charters and fundamental laws. Everywhere it means
20 change and trouble.
    We are convinced that society can no longer be saved without strong and vigorous resolutions on the part of the Governments still free in their opinions and actions.... The first principle to be followed by the monarchs, united as they are by the coincidence of their desires and
25 opinions, should be that of maintaining the stability of political institutions against the disorganised excitement which has taken possession of men's minds; the immutability of principles against the madness of their interpretation; and respect for laws actually in force against a desire for their destruction ...

The Tsar was in sympathy with Metternich's beliefs and put forward a proposal at the Congress that Russia, Austria and Prussia should agree to act jointly, using force if necessary, to restore any government which had itself been overthrown by force. The proposal was accepted and, in the Protocol of Troppau, the three Great Powers announced that they 'would never recognise the rights of a people to restrict the powers of their King'. This ran directly contrary to the ambitions of liberals and nationalists everywhere, and was particularly disappointing to those in the German states. Prussia as well as Austria was firmly ranged on the side of reaction. Old rivalries between the two Powers, which had resulted in two major wars in the eighteenth century, were forgotten. Both worked closely together to preserve the status quo.

As well as the weapons of diplomacy and threats of force, Metternich used those of the police state to maintain the status quo. A special office was set up in Vienna to open, copy and then reseal foreign correspondence passing through Austria. This gave him an enormous amount of secret information about the activities of other governments and it was backed up by reports from his network of spies throughout Europe and by the work of his secret police. By a combination of repression and press censorship in individual states, and a system of international alliances to preserve peace, Metternich hoped to keep Europe quiet and to allow revolutionary fervour to simmer down. Throughout the 1820s he was generally successful.

ACTIVITY

Read carefully the extracts from Metternich's secret memorandum. Answer the following questions:
a) What does Metternich mean when he uses the phrases 'pure monarchies' and 'the immutability of principles'?
b) Metternich argues that there must be no change in political institutions. What arguments does he use to support his point of view?

---

c) The 1830s

In the 1830s the picture changed. The July Revolution in Paris in 1830, followed by the successful Belgian revolt against Dutch rule, sparked off demonstrations and riots in several south German states. The demands were for a constitution as laid down in the Federal Act of 1815, which had set up the Confederation; or, if a constitution already existed, for its liberalisation. In Brunswick the Duke was driven out and his successor was forced to grant a more liberal constitution. In both Saxony and Hesse-Cassel similar concessions were obtained. In Bavaria, Baden and Württemberg, where constitutions already existed, liberal opposition parties gained parliamentary seats in new elections, and greater freedom of the press allowed criticisms of the government.

In the early 1830s a number of republican groups were busy with plans for the unification of Germany. In 1832 25,000 nationalists met at the Hambach Festival in Bavaria to drink, talk and plan revolution. The tricolour flag, symbol of revolution, was hoisted and toasts drunk to the notion that power – sovereignty – should lie with the people.

Metternich, not surprisingly, was thrown into a panic. In the same year, with Prussian support, he persuaded the Diet to pass the Six Articles. These increased its control over the internal affairs of individual states, and forbade political associations and popular meetings. The effect was to make the Diet hated by nationalists everywhere in the Confederation, and in 1833 armed students tried to take it over. The rising was quickly defeated and the Diet set up a special commission to round up young student agitators, many of whom were forming themselves into a 'Young Germany' movement. This movement was dedicated to establishing a united Germany based on liberal principles, international peace and free love. Faced with such developments, Metternich again summoned representatives from the Confederation to meet him in Vienna in 1834 to discuss the need for yet sterner action against subversive elements. Press censorship was intensified and new controls placed on universities.

4 Economic Developments

> **KEY ISSUE** To what extent did economic developments
> encourage German unity?

Few liberals in the period 1815–48 would have foreseen that the nationalist aim of the political unification of Germany would eventually be brought about by Prussia, one of the most reactionary of the German states; nor if they had, would they have been best pleased by the manner of its doing. Nevertheless, the basis for the unification of Germany had already been laid by Prussia before 1840, and that basis, which was not political but economic, was the *Zollverein*.

a) The Prussian Customs Union

After 1815 the 39 German states managed their own economies. Innumerable customs barriers and internal tariffs restricted trade. Even within a single state there were large numbers of tolls. Variations in currency values within the Confederation were an added problem. The silver thaler, the main unit of coinage, varied in value from state to state.

In 1818 Rhineland manufacturers complained to the King of Prussia about the massive burden on home industry, and about competition from unrestricted foreign imports, on which no duty was charged. As a result, in the same year, the Prussian Tariff Reform Law brought into being the Prussian Customs Union. The law did away with the web of internal customs duties and replaced them by a tariff to be charged at the Prussian state frontier. However, the Customs Union was not quite what the Rhineland industrialists sought: they had hoped for a high protective tariff, particularly against British goods. Instead, the tariff was low: nothing at all on raw materials, an average of 10 per cent on manufactured goods and 20 per cent on luxury goods such as sugar or tea. High tariffs would only have encouraged smuggling, which was already widespread. Nor was Prussia economically or politically strong enough to engage in a tariff war with other countries, who would only have put high duties on Prussian exports in return. Later Prussia did introduce customs duties on raw materials, especially iron and cotton yarn imported from Britain, as it tried to protect home industry from foreign competition. Nevertheless (and at the same time), it was working to extend free trade, first within Prussia and then within other states in the Confederation, by getting rid of as many internal trade barriers as possible so that goods would move more freely. This meant wider markets for home produced goods at cheaper prices.

Some of Prussia's smaller neighbours were so impressed by its economic success that they agreed to join a customs union with Prussia, and even allowed Prussian customs officers into their territories to operate the system. In 1828 one of the larger neighbouring states, Hesse-Darmstadt, also signed a customs treaty with Prussia.

By 1830 customs unions were proliferating. As well as the Prussian-Hesse-Darmstadt union, there were two others. One was between Bavaria and Württemberg; the other, known as the Middle German Commercial Union, was made up of Hanover, Brunswick, Saxony and several smaller states. This Union was not quite like the others, for it was not so much concerned with encouraging its own trade as spoiling that of Prussia. Prussia was geographically well placed to control north–south routes through north Germany and to generate a large income out of duties charged on foreign goods carried along these routes. The Middle Union worked to protect and keep open the existing roads from the North Sea ports to the central German cities of Frankfurt and Leipzig and to build a series of new roads which would go round the states of the Prussian Customs Union. In this scheme they were thwarted by the Prussian Finance Minister, who encouraged the building of roads joining Prussia directly with Bavaria, Württemberg and Frankfurt. He also extended Prussian trade along the Rhine through a customs agreement with the Dutch.

b) The Zollverein

In 1830 Hesse-Cassel, one of the smaller but vitally important states of the Middle Union, ran into financial difficulties and revolutionary upheavals. The following year she joined the Prussian Customs Union – to the horror of her Middle Union partners. The Middle Union, which was already in trouble, collapsed soon after, while the Prussian

Customs Union went from strength to strength. In 1834 Bavaria and Württemberg joined the Prussians, and this new enlarged Customs Union, the *Zollverein*, covered 18 states with 23 million people. By 1844 only Hanover, Oldenburg, Mecklenburg, the Hanseatic towns and Austria were not members. The *Zollverein* promised for all member states a common system of customs and tariffs, and the abolition of all internal customs barriers. Each state had the right to appoint some officials to the customs departments of other states, and as long as they did not break the rules of the *Zollverein* each state could negotiate its own trade treaties. The organisation and supervision of the *Zollverein* was carried out by a specially appointed body, the *Zollverein* Congress. In the next few years a start was made on unifying both the currency and the system of weights and measures in the states of the *Zollverein*. The railways were greatly extended to make a quick and efficient means of communication between its members.

There were some difficulties. The *Zollverein* administration did not always work smoothly, and as any member state could veto a proposal at the *Zollverein* Congress, decisions were often held up or not made at all. Nevertheless, the experiment of the *Zollverein* was generally successful, certainly from Prussia's point of view. The member states worked together and Prussia achieved a position of economic leadership within the Confederation. Moreover, the *Zollverein* became a focal point for national feeling, and when in 1844 it signed a favourable trade treaty with Belgium, it could be said to speak for the major part of the Confederation in international economic affairs.

What was Prussia's aim in setting up the *Zollverein*? Successive Prussian Finance Ministers realised that doing away with internal customs duties, first within Prussia, and then between Prussia and neighbouring states, would increase trade and bring prosperity. It would also help unite Prussia with her distant Rhineland territories. As early as 1830, even before the *Zollverein* was formed, the Prussian Finance Minister had pointed out to his King that such a free trade organisation would not only bring prosperity to Prussia and her associates, but would isolate Austria. This isolation would not only be economic but would eventually weaken her political influence within the Confederation. Many modern historians support the view that from the 1830s onwards Prussia was using the *Zollverein* to achieve 'a Prussian solution to the German question'. The argument is that those who found financial advantage in an economic union under Prussian leadership might be expected to take a favourable view of similar arrangements in a political union. The *Zollverein* was a force for unity in the 1840s and therefore a focal point for nationalist sentiments. As a result, Prussia, despite her reactionary political sympathies, came to be regarded by many northern states as the natural leader of a united Germany.

Why did Austria stay outside the *Zollverein*? She had refused to join at the beginning, because she disagreed with the policy of free trade. Austria's policy was protectionist. She already had large markets within the Austrian Empire for her home produced goods, and therefore wanted high import duties to protect her industries and markets from cheap foreign imports. Joining the *Zollverein* would have meant reducing her import duties to the same level as the other states, and this she would not consider. Only if the *Zollverein* raised the general level of tariffs would Austria join, and this Prussia in turn would not consider. Austria gave Prussia a great opportunity when she refused to join. Prussia took it, established her position of leadership, and made sure that Austria would stay outside. By 1848, if Austria still retained political control of the Confederation, Prussia had the economic leadership.

5 Nationalist and Liberal Development by the 1840s

> **KEY ISSUE** How strong were German nationalist and liberal movements before 1848?

a) The Growth of Nationalism

The emotional appeal of nationalism was experienced by increasing numbers of Germans after 1815. It was based on the twin themes of hatred of France and a highly coloured view of Germany's great, and as yet unfulfilled, role in Europe. It was fuelled by several situations in which foreign governments appeared to threaten Germany as a whole, and which made many Germans, who were normally content to think of themselves as Prussians, Bavarians, Hessians or members of other states, discontented that Germany could not speak with a single, strong voice at times of crisis. These feelings were particularly widespread in 1840 when it seemed likely that France would invade the German states along the Rhine in an attempt to force the other major powers to bow to her wishes over a crisis in the Near East. The German press threw its weight behind the nationalist upsurge and there was a flurry of songs and poems such as *Deutschland über Alles* ('Germany above the others', which eventually became Germany's national anthem). In the end France backed down, but not before much nationalistic feeling had been generated throughout Germany in the face of a threat from the 'old enemy'.

It is easy to understand why a threat from France should evoke such a response. After all, only 25 years had elapsed since the final defeat of Napoleon. Less immediately understandable is the reaction to action from Denmark, which was relatively small, weak and internationally insignificant. Yet in 1846 Denmark did as much to create support for the idea of German unification as had France in 1840. Immediately to the south of Denmark proper lay the duchies of Schleswig and Holstein. They were ruled over by the King of Denmark and were a part of his kingdom in all but name. Schleswig was half German and half Danish-speaking and was not a member of the German Confederation. Holstein, by contrast, had an over-whelmingly German-speaking population and was one of the member states of the Confederation. When it seemed that the King of Denmark was about to incorporate Schleswig and Holstein into his kingdom, the outcry throughout Germany was enormous. What to most people throughout Europe, including the King of Denmark, seemed merely a legal technicality was viewed by most Germans as a violation of the Fatherland to be resisted by force if need be. Bavarian, Prussian and Austrian leaders all spoke against the Danish action. This strength of feeling was enough to persuade the King of Denmark to abandon his plans.

Another factor of great significance in the development of nation-alism was the coming of the railway. One German economist described the growing railway network as 'the firm girdle around the loins of Germany binding her limbs together into a forceful and powerful body'. The railways certainly made Germans more mobile and may well have contributed to the breakdown of local and regional barriers. Along with the development of a telegraph system and improved methods of printing which reduced the cost of newspapers, railways also helped the spread of – German – news.

b) The Growth of Liberalism

The 1840s were also to bring new and hopeful developments for liberals. In the south-western states the liberals increased their popu-lar support. In Baden half the elected members of the Lower House of Parliament were government officials who had been converted to liberalism. When two of them were suspended in 1843, it led to a vote of no confidence in the government and its eventual defeat. Three years later the liberals in Baden managed to obtain a relaxation of press censorship, and reforms of the police and of the judicial system. In Hesse-Darmstadt there were strong liberal parliamentary cam-paigns for changes in electoral rules and for a free press. In Bavaria the liberals were helped by an unexpected change of policy on the part of the half-mad King, Ludwig I. His passion for a dancer led him to propose that she should be given a title and land. When his advis-ers criticised him, he dismissed the government and replaced his reactionary ministers with liberal ones.

Developments in Prussia also seemed promising. King Frederick William III, who had ruled as an absolute monarch for over 40 years, died in 1840. Although he had agreed to the establishment of provin-cial Diets in 1823, he had avoided granting a constitution, partly because it was against his inclination to do so, and partly because he had been heavily pressurised by Austria. Throughout his reign he had close ties with Austria. He was succeeded by his son Frederick William IV – an intelligent, cultured but very unstable man whose policies were to fluctuate widely throughout his reign. Sometimes he behaved as a reactionary absolutist, sometimes as a constitutional monarch. He started by acting as many liberals wished him to. He released many political prisoners, relaxed press censorship and appointed a leading liberal to the Council of State. In 1842 he arranged for the eight provincial Diets to elect representatives to meet as an advisory body on a temporary basis in Berlin. He extended the powers of the provincial Diets and allowed them to publish reports of their debates.

Encouraged by this, middle-class liberals began to agitate for a constitution and the calling of a single Diet or Parliament for all Prussian territories. The conservative landed aristocracy of Prussia, the Junkers, watched the activities of the King with anxiety and even considered a coup to replace him with his brother, William.

Frederick William, taking fright at finding himself under political attack from both left and right, reimposed press censorship in 1843. However, in 1847 he called a meeting of the United Diet in Berlin to vote a loan for building a railway to link East Prussia and Berlin. Liberal hopes that this was the fulfilment of their demand for a single Diet for all Prussia were soon dashed, for the United Diet refused to grant the loan for the railway and was soon dispersed. The liberals renewed their demands for a national assembly of the kind promised in the Vienna Settlement, but the King refused. He would go no further towards granting a constitution.

c) Conclusion

In the 1840s the pace of political debate picked up and public opinion grew bolder. More books were published. Newspapers and political journals flourished. The fact that Germans were the most literate people in Europe helped. Popular journals played a crucial role in arousing interest in issues such as Schleswig-Holstein in 1846. In 1847 liberal and nationalist sentiments found expression in the foundation at Heidelberg of a newspaper with the prophetic title of *Die Deutsche Zeitung* (The German Newspaper). Equally important was a meeting of liberal representatives of the south-western states at Hippenhelm. They drew up a programme of reform, demanded an elected national Diet and detailed their complaints which were published in *Die Deutsche Zeitung.*

1 The Diet has so far not fulfilled the tasks set it by the Act of the Confederation in the fields of representation by estates, free trade, communications, navigation, freedom of the press etc; the federal defence regulation provides neither for the arming of the population
5 nor for a uniformly organised federal force. On the contrary the press is harassed by censorship; the discussions of the Diet are enveloped in secrecy. ... The only expression of the common German interests in

existence, the Customs Union, was not created by the Confederation,
but negotiated outside its framework, through treaties between indi-
10 vidual states; negotiations about a German law on bills of exchange, and
about a postal union, are conducted not by the Confederation but by
the several governments . . . .The liberation of the press, . . . open and
oral judicial proceedings with juries, separation of the executive and
judicial powers, transfer to the courts of the administration of the
15 laws . . ., drafting of a police criminal code, freeing the soil and its tillers
from medieval burdens, independence of the communes in the administration of their affairs, reduction of the cost of the standing army and
establishments of a national guard etc. were discussed at length, as were
the constitutional means that could be used to give force to the just
20 demands of the people. Particular attention was given to possible ways
of reducing impoverishment and want and, a closely related topic, of
reforming the system of taxation . . .

ACTIVITY

Read the extract from the report of the Hippenheim meeting in
Die Deutsche Zeitung. Answer the following questions.
a) Is the Diet mainly criticised for what it has done or for what it
has not done?
b) What evidence does the report contain to suggest that those
who met at Hippenheim were German nationalists?
c) What evidence does the report contain to suggest that those
who met at Hippenheim belonged to the middle classes?

The *Zollverein*'s example of economic co-operation between the
German states encouraged the liberals and nationalists. It made their
dreams of a politically united Germany seem more likely to be
realised. On a practical level the states of the *Zollverein* had prospered
– would not the same be true following political unity? Liberal
nationalists pointed out the savings which could be made by doing
away with 39 separate states, governments, legal systems, administra-
tions and embassies, and replacing them with a central government.
By the late 1840s there was a growing feeling that the German nation
was a fact and a growing call for its political realisation in the setting
up of a nation state. The greatest support for nationalism and liberalism came from the middle classes. Most liberal-nationalists envisaged
a federation of states under a constitutional monarch. Suspicious of
full democracy, they wanted to limit the vote to the prosperous and
well-educated. Radicals, by contrast, favoured universal manhood suffrage and pressed for a German republic.

However, it is wrong to over-estimate the degree of political consciousness attained by Germans on the eve of the 1848 revolutions.
Even among the middle classes only a minority were liberal-minded

and an even smaller minority were politically active. Most liberals were concerned with developments in their own states, not in the situation across Germany as a whole. Small in number and far from unified, they were also isolated from the mass of the people. In truth, nationalists, liberals and radicals had achieved very little by 1848. As long as Metternich remained in power and Prussia remained Austria's ally, there seemed little chance of changing the situation. German nationalism as a mass phenomenon tended to be reactive, erupting in response to perceived threats and then subsiding again. Although nationalist organisations such as the Gymnasts Movement, choral societies and shooting clubs grew at an impressive rate in the mid-1840s, loyalty to individual states and dynasties remained strong. There was still a major division between the Catholic south which looked to Austria and the Protestant north which looked to Prussia. There were also cultural differences between the more industrialised and liberal west and the agrarian, autocratic east.

Summary Diagram
Germany, 1815–1848

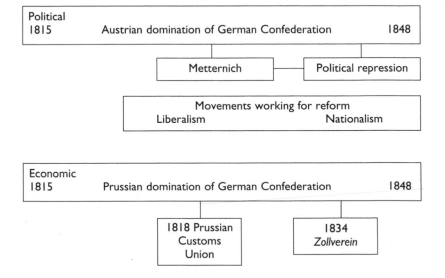

Working on Chapter 1

By now you should have an understanding of how much progress Germany had made on the road to national unity in the early nineteenth century. Clearly, Germany was more united in 1848 than she had been in 1800. There were far fewer states. The German Confederation of 1815, although usually criticised by contemporary German nationalists and by historians since, at least provided a framework within which German states co-existed. There is evidence that German national feeling was growing. The *Zollverein* seems to have helped to promote the idea of German unification. These are the positive points. Now make a list of the negative points. What had not been achieved? What obstacles still stood in the way of national unity?

Answering structured and essay questions on Chapter 1

It is likely that you will use information from this chapter to answer general questions on the unification of Germany. The one topic from the period which may well appear as a fairly self-contained issue is the *Zollverein*. Consider the following question:

Examine the causes of the formation of the *Zollverein* and its results for Prussia, Austria and the German states.

Make a list of the points you would use to explain a) the causes and b) the consequences of the *Zollverein*. Keep the list and add to it once you have read chapter 3. Look at the points on your list. For each one decide whether the words 'economic' or 'political' describe it best. Put 'E' or 'P' against each one. Where you are tempted to put down both 'E' and 'P' rethink the point and if possible divide it into two. By grouping the 'E' and 'P' points together you should have ready a four part plan to answer the question.

Source-based questions on Chapter 1

Study the following sources and then answer the questions which follow.

Source A: Extracts from the Carlsbad Decrees (1819)

THE PRESS LAW
As long as the present decree shall be in force, no daily paper or pamphlet of less than twenty sheets shall be issued from the press without the previous consent of the public authority.

LAW ESTABLISHING A CENTRAL COMMISSION OF INVESTI-
GATION
1. Within fourteen days from the date of this decree, an extraordinary
commission of enquiry, appointed by the Diet and composed of seven
members, including the president, shall assemble in the city of Mainz.
2. The object of this commission is to make careful and detailed
enquiries respecting the facts, the origin and the multifarious ramifica-
tions of the secret revolutionary activities and demagogic associations,
directed against the political constitution and internal repose of the
confederation ...

Source B: Part of a secret memorandum sent by Metternich to Tsar
Alexander 1 of Russia in 1819.

1 In short, let the great monarchs strengthen their union, and prove to
   the world that if it exists, it is beneficent, and ensures the political peace
   of Europe; that it is powerful only for the maintenance of tranquillity at
   a time when so many attacks are directed against it; that the principles
5 which they profess are paternal and protective, menacing only disturbers of public tranquillity.

Source C: Metternich to the American G. Licknor

1 It is true that I do not like democracies. Democracy is in every case a
   principle of dissolution, of decomposition. It tends to separate men, it
   loosens society. I am opposed to this because I am by nature and by
   habit constructive. That is why monarchy is the only government that
5 suits my way of thinking ... Monarchy alone tends to bring men
   together, to unite them in compact, efficient masses, and to make them
   capable by their combined efforts of the highest degree of culture and
   civilisation.

1. Study Source B and use your own knowledge.
   What did Metternich mean when he wrote about 'the disturbers of
   public tranquillity'? (3 marks)
2. Compare Sources A, B and C and use your own knowledge.
   Comment on the usefulness of the three sources in terms of explaining
   Metternich's 'System'. (7 marks)
3. Study all three Sources and use your own knowledge.
   How important was Metternich in preventing the creation of a German
   nation? (15 marks)

2 Germany in Revolution, 1848-49

POINTS TO CONSIDER

In 1848 France, the German Confederation, Habsburg lands including Austria and Hungary, and Italy experienced revolution. A striking feature of the revolutions, both in Germany and elsewhere, was the rapidity of the success they enjoyed. Another striking feature was the fact that all – equally rapidly – failed. The revolutions are complex affairs. Some historians claim that general – European-wide – factors explain the cause, course and failure of the revolutions. Others stress that revolutionaries in different areas had very different grievances and demands. Even within specific countries, there was often little cohesion among the revolutionaries and what there was soon collapsed. Given this ongoing debate, three questions arise:
– What factors helped spark revolution in many Germany states?
– Was there a common theme to the German revolutions?
– Why did the revolutions fail?

KEY DATES:

1848 **March 5** Declaration of Heidelberg.
Mid-March Riots in Berlin.
Late March King Frederick William made concessions to liberal opposition.
March 31 Meeting of the Vorparlament.
May Meeting of Prussian and Frankfurt Parliaments.
November Frederick William re-established control in Berlin.
December New Prussian constitution.
1849 **March** Frankfurt Parliament agreed on a constitution.
April Frederick William rejected the offer of the German crown.
June Frankfurt Parliament finally dispersed.

1 The Causes of the German Revolutions

> **KEY ISSUE** What caused the German revolutions?

a) Introduction

1848 was a year to remember in Europe, a year of dramatic, violent events, of hope and of failure. It was the year of death in the cholera epidemic, which swept across Europe, causing such loss of life that for a while society in many areas was totally disorganised. It was the year that Karl Marx's *Communist Manifesto* was published. This did not have the drama of the cholera epidemic and attracted little attention at the time, but its message later spread across Europe and beyond to become, a century later, the basis of the political system of half the world. In the spring of 1848 revolutionaries, to the delight of Marx, seemed to carry all before them across Europe. By the start of 1849, however, it was clear that the high hopes had not been realised.

Why did revolutions in France, Germany, Prussia, Austria, Hungary and Italy all happen in the same year? Historians used to think that the French troubles, which began in Paris in February 1848, simply triggered off copy-cat revolutions in other countries. Now a generally accepted view is that the revolutions took place at about the same time because conditions across Europe were all very similar. These conditions – economic, social and political – are seen as giving rise to revolutions. The sections that follow focus on Germany. However, much – indeed most – of what is said applies to many parts of Europe.

b) Long-term Economic and Social Problems

Most historians agree that the German revolutions resulted, at least in part, from social and economic crisis. However, the precise nature of this crisis, and its effects on different classes of the population, has generated much debate.

Since the middle of the eighteenth century, Germany's (like Europe's) population had grown dramatically, doubling in the century up to 1848, and increasing from 24 to 36 million between 1816 and 1848. The reasons for this increase are not certain. Economic historians tend to the view that it was more probably due to a declining death rate than to an increasing birth rate. Whatever the cause, the result was that some areas found it difficult to sustain their populations. Thus people left the land and drifted to the towns in search of work or went to other parts of the world, especially the United States, hoping to better themselves. Those who remained in the countryside found life very hard. Many German peasants still owed feudal dues to great landowners. In eastern Prussia much of the land belonged to the *Junkers*, the landowning military aristocracy, and was worked by landless peasants. Even in the parts of Germany where the peasants had become tenant farmers rents were very high. It was difficult to make a living. Many peasants, therefore, were restless and resentful.

In most towns there were insufficient jobs and housing to cope with the influx of migrants from the countryside. (The population of Berlin, for example, grew by 100,000 in the 1840s.) Living conditions were often atrocious. Even in good times workers were poorly housed, clothed and fed. Working conditions were also grim. The machines, especially in the textile factories, were not designed with the workers in mind. Men, women and children worked for 13 hours a day, often in cramped and awkward positions, crouched over the machines. This led to deformities of one kind or another among many of the workers. Many newcomers, unable to find work, depended on charity or turned to crime. Strikes and riots amongst the urban working class multiplied in the 1830s and 1840s. Towns had concentrations of discontented people who were far more likely to act together than their rural counterparts. It is worth noting that the 1848 revolutions in Germany were overwhelmingly urban, particularly occurring in capital cities like Berlin and Vienna.

Across Germany industry was growing in the early nineteenth century. Although large-scale factories were still uncommon, skilled artisans felt threatened by the advance of mechanisation which forced down the costs of production and made hand-produced goods relatively expensive.

Historians remain divided about whether 'class consciousness' was developing among industrial workers. Karl Marx, a German revolutionary, argued that as industrialisation developed so each class evolved its own consciousness. He believed that the working class (or proletariat) was inevitably opposed to the upper and middle classes (or bourgeoisie) who owned the means of production (factories, mills, mines, etc.). Marx, and Marxist historians since, argued that the 1848 revolutions were caused by the effect of industrialisation on the working class. Certainly, in Germany (like elsewhere) it was often workers who fought and died in the streets behind the barricades. However, it was not only the workers who made the German revolutions. Others played an important part, particularly the educated middle classes. Moreover, Marxist historians find it hard to explain why, if working-class consciousness was so important, revolution did not occur in Britain in 1848. Britain was far more industrialised than Germany at this time and working-class consciousness was far stronger.

c) The Economic Crisis: 1845–8

The 1846 harvest was bad, resulting in disastrous consequences in 1847, and the situation was made worse by a serious outbreak of potato blight. (Potatoes were the main item of diet for most German peasants.) There was distress and unrest, and food riots broke out. There had been poor harvests before, but the increased population made the position worse.

The industrial towns also felt the pressure on food supplies, and there was a sharp rise in food prices. Cereal prices increased by nearly 50 per cent in 1847. In Berlin, the so-called 'potato revolution' occurred. Barricades were erected, shops looted and the Crown Prince's palace stormed before soldiers managed to restore order. Across Germany, the rise in food prices in 1846–7 led to a sharp reduction in consumer spending on items other than foodstuffs. Consequently, craft and industrial production suffered a steep fall in demand, to which merchants and employers responded by cancelling orders and laying off workers. There was thus a rapid increase in unemployment, particularly in the textile industry. Even those in work found their wages cut. Most workers' standard of living fell alarmingly as higher food prices coincided with lower wages. Cheap alcohol gave some comfort in a hard life, and contemporary writers describe the great increase in drunkenness, especially among women and children factory workers.

In both town and country, among workers and peasants, there was growing unrest. Dissatisfied with the existing state of affairs, they demanded a better life for themselves and their families with enough food, reasonable housing, a shorter working day and improved working conditions. Most were concerned with practical matters, not politics and political theories. There were some exceptions. In towns like Cologne and Bonn, skilled craftsmen had their own trade organisations, and kept themselves apart from the unskilled factory workers, whom they both despised and feared. The leaders of the skilled workers were often articulate and politically aware. During 1848 they staged demonstrations and elected representative assemblies to discuss their grievances. The assembly, or congress, held at Frankfurt drew up an Industrial Code to regulate hours of work, rates of pay and so on. (They later presented the Code to the Frankfurt Parliament for approval but it was turned down.) At the time of the riots in Berlin in March 1848 some politically active workers organised themselves into Workers' Committees, demanding among other things the formation of trades unions, free education and a guaranteed minimum wage.

d) Political Problems

The economic crisis helped to shake the prestige and self-confidence of many existing regimes which lacked the financial and bureaucratic resources – and also possibly the will – to intervene effectively to alleviate the social distress and reverse the economic collapse. The calibre of rulers was not high and many monarchs and their ministers attracted a great deal of personal unpopularity, particularly from the growing number of the educated middle class – lawyers, doctors, journalists, teachers and civil servants – frustrated by their lack of power. In 1848 power lay where it always had, with the nobility. They filled senior government jobs, officered the army, and guarded their privileges jealously against any infiltration by the middle classes. Middle-class Germans were critical of systems which largely excluded them from participation in the political process, and in which they were restrained from free expression of their grievances by the censor and the secret police.

The new political ideas of liberalism and nationalism, which were developing during the first half of the nineteenth century, proved increasingly attractive to the dissatisfied middle classes. Many wanted the elimination of arbitrary government, the establishment of some form of parliamentary system and the guarantee of basic civil rights. They also wanted to see the establishment of a united Germany which they claimed would ensure national prosperity. By 1847 patriotism was running high, and the feelings of many Germans were expressed in a memorandum written by Prince Hohenlohe:

1 In the history of every nation there is an epoch in which it comes to full self consciousness and claims liberty to determine its own destiny. ... We Germans have reached this stage. The nation demands a share in public administration as never before. ... No one will deny that it is

5 hard on an energetic thinking man to be unable to say abroad 'I am a German' – not to be able to pride himself that the German flag is flying from his vessel, to have no German consul in case of emergency, but have to explain 'I am a Hessian, a Darmstadter, a Buckeburger; my fatherland was once a great and powerful country, now it is shattered

10 into nine and thirty splinters.'

The impetus for a German national revolution came surprisingly from the small, and hitherto undistinguished, state of Baden in south-west Germany. In 1846 the Grand Duke of Baden had been forced to accept a liberal constitution. In consequence, the Baden representative assembly was elected on a wider franchise than in any other German state. Not surprisingly, the people of Baden were more politically conscious than most Germans. Throughout the 1840s liberal politicians in Baden had been proposing a united Germany instead of the loose Confederation. Now they put their views forcefully to an assembly of liberals from all the south-west German states (see page 22). This assembly, which met in October 1847, agreed on the urgent need for an independent German People's Parliament.

While this meeting was going on, radical politicians were holding their own meetings in south-west Germany, and again proceedings were dominated by the representatives from Baden. The radicals wanted fairer taxation, education for all, a people's army, better relations between employees and workers and, most important, the establishment of a united German Republic.

e) The Situation in early 1848

In 1848 few Germans actually expected revolution. There was still widespread loyalty to the established dynasties. Moreover, the economic situation was beginning to improve slightly. Nevertheless, economic distress in the major cities, which continued over the winter of 1847–8, helped foment revolution, encouraging subversive propaganda, undermining the credit of the states, and unifying the discontented.

2 The Impact of Revolution

KEY ISSUE How and why was the Frankfurt Parliament created?

---

a) The start of Revolution

On 24 February 1848 King Louis-Philippe was overthrown and a republic was established in France. French revolutionaries' proclamation of the idea of the sovereignty of the people called in question all established authority. News of events in France helped spark revolution in many small south-west German states, which then spread north. News of Metternich's fall from power in Vienna on 13 March 1848 had a profound psychological effect on Germans and added fuel to the revolutionary conflagration. In some places, peasants attacked their landlords, stormed castles and destroyed feudal records. Elsewhere artisans used the opportunity of the breakdown of law and order to destroy new machines which they saw as a threat to their livelihood. In Baden radical republicans tried to lead a peasant and worker rising. This attracted little support and was quickly suppressed by the liberal government. Meetings, demonstrations and petitions, not armed risings, were the chief weapons of the middle-class revolutionaries who hoped to work with and not destroy the princes. Most German rulers lost their nerve, giving in easily if temporarily, to demands for more representative government. In Austria, for example, Emperor Ferdinand agreed to summon a constituent assembly to draw up a new constitution. Faced with serious revolts in Italy, Hungary and Bohemia, Austria was too engrossed in its own affairs in the spring and summer of 1848 to exert its customary influence on Germany. Events in Berlin in March 1848 prevented Prussian King Frederick William from taking action against the revolutionaries.

For a time the revolutionary fire seemed irresistible because no one was fighting it. But although the eccentric Bavarian King Ludwig was forced to abdicate (largely because of a scandal over the Irish-born dancer Lola Montez, with whom the King was infatuated), in most states the old rulers survived and watched developments.

b) The Vorparlament

In March 1848, at a meeting in Heidelberg, representatives from six states discussed changes to Germany's political institutions. They did so before revolutions had made an impact on Germany. On 5 March their decisions were published in the Declaration of Heidelberg:

1 Heidelberg, 5th March. Today fifty-one men were assembled here, from Prussia, Bavaria, Württemberg, Baden, Nassau and Frankfurt, almost all members of state assemblies, in order to discuss the most urgent measures for the Fatherland in this moment of decision.

5 Unanimously resolved in their devotion to the freedom, unity, independence and honour of the German nation, they all express their conviction that the establishment and defence of these highest blessings must be attempted by co-operation of all the German peoples with their governments, so long as delivery is still possible in this manner ...

10 The assembled unanimously expressed their conviction of what the Fatherland urgently needs as follows:

'Germany must not be involved in war through intervention in the affairs of the neighbouring country or through non-recognition of the changes in the state made there.

15 Germans must not be caused to diminish or rob from other nations the freedom and independence which they themselves ask as their right.

The meeting of a national representation elected in all the German lands according to the number of the people must not be postponed, both for the removal of imminent internal and external dangers, and for
20 the development of the strength and flowering of German national life!'

At the same time they have agreed to concentrate their efforts so that as soon as possible a more complete assembly of men of trust from all German peoples should come together in order to continue deliberation of this most important matter and to offer its co-operation to the
25 Fatherland as well as to the Governments. To this end seven members were requested to prepare proposals concerning the election and the establishment of an appropriate national representation and speedily to take care of the invitations to an assembly of German men.

A main task of the national representation will in any case be common
30 defence ... and external representation, whereby great sums of money will be saved for other important needs, while at the same time the identity and suitable self-administration of the different states remains in existence.

ACTIVITY

Read carefully the extracts from the Declaration of Heidelberg. Answer the following questions:
a) What policies did the authors favour in foreign affairs?
b) What was the attitude of the Declaration's authors towards the existing governments of the German states? Explain your answer.
c) What evidence suggests that that the delegates were generally conservative in economic and social matters?

Invitations for the proposed 'assembly of German men' were quickly issued. This move, which looked directly to the German people for support, was unexpectedly successful. On 31 March over 500 representatives, from almost all the states of the Confederation (but mainly from the south and west), squeezed themselves into the pews of the *Pauluskirche* (St. Paul's Church) in Frankfurt. This assembly is known as the *Vorparlament*. This is usually translated as 'pre-Parliament', but it is better thought of as 'preparatory Parliament', which was preparing the way for the real Parliament. After five days of debate, the *Vorparlament* members reached an agreement on how to elect a national Parliament which would draw up a constitution for a united Germany.

It was decided that the Parliament, which would meet in Frankfurt, should consist of one representative for every 50,000 inhabitants and be elected by citizens, who were of age and 'economically independent'. It was left to individual states to decide who was an independent citizen. Most states decided on a residence qualification, some on ownership of property. Although the *Vorparlament* did not actually say so, it was assumed that only men could vote, so women were excluded from the franchise along with servants, farm labourers and anyone receiving poor relief. This last category alone excluded large numbers: in Cologne, for example, nearly a third of the population was on poor relief.

c) The Frankfurt Parliament

The elections, arranged at short notice and in all 39 states, were carried out peacefully and successfully. More people were able to vote than could vote in British elections at this time. However, in most of the states the elections were indirect. The voters elected 'electors', who in their turn chose representatives. The Parliament, which met in Frankfurt in May 1848, was not very representative of the population as a whole. Of the 596 members, the vast majority were middle-class-teachers, professors, lawyers and government officials. It was probably the best-educated Parliament ever – over 80 per cent of the members held university degrees, mostly in law. There were a few landowners, four craftsmen and one peasant.

However, it had been a great achievement to have got the Frankfurt Parliament elected, convened and ready to begin work in only a little over a month. The Parliament also started with the advantage that the old Diet of the Confederation, with representatives appointed by new liberal governments, had agreed to its own demise and nominated the Parliament as its legal successor. The key issue was whether it would be able to draw up a national constitution which would be accepted by all Germans. The Parliament was essentially moderate and liberal: only a small minority of its members were radical, revolutionary or republican. It intended to establish a united

Germany under a constitutional monarch who would rule through an elected Parliament. Apart from drawing up a national constitution, it hoped to agree a series of 'Basic Rights and Demands', such as freedom of the press, fair taxation, equality of political rights without regard to religion and separation of Church and State.

The Parliament started by considering the relationship between itself and the individual states. The Confederation had been an association in which the states had a very large degree of independence from federal control. The Frankfurt Parliament's intention was that the new 'Germany' should have much stronger central government, with correspondingly greater control over the actions of the states. It quickly decided that any national constitution which it framed would be sovereign, and that while state parliaments would be free to make state laws, they would only be valid if they did not conflict with that constitution. So by the end of May the Frankfurt Parliament had declared its authority over the states, their parliaments and Princes. Now it remained to draw up a constitution and to organise a government.

Most members of the Parliament could accept that the logical approach would be to agree a constitution and then to set up a government according to its terms. But it was another matter to find a majority of members who favoured any one procedure for carrying out these tasks, or who shared similar views on the details of the constitution to be established. Without the discipline imposed by well-organised political parties and without the dominance provided by outstanding leaders, the Frankfurt Parliament became a 'talking shop' in which it was difficult to reach agreement on anything.

Once it became clear that it would not be possible to reach rapid agreement on a constitution, steps were taken to establish a provisional government to rule in the meantime. But so little was agreed about the specific ways in which its powers were to be carried out that the 'Provisional Central Power' established at the end of June was largely ineffectual.

The Provisional Central Power provided for an Imperial Regent, or Vicar of the Empire, to be elected by the Parliament. He was to govern through ministers, appointed by him and responsible to Parliament, until such time as a decision about the constitution could be reached. An elderly Austrian Archduke, John, was elected as Regent. He was an unusual Archduke, married to the daughter of a village postmaster, and with known liberal views and German nationalist sympathies. He duly appointed a number of ministers but, as they did not have any staff or offices or money, and their duties were not clearly defined, they could do little.

As the summer went on, it seemed less and less likely that the Confederation would be transformed into a united Germany by the efforts of the Frankfurt Parliament. Nevertheless, the Parliament did not give up and continued its interminable debate over the constitution. In fairness to the delegates, there seemed no great need for speed. The important thing was to get it right.

In December, the Fifty Articles of the fundamental rights of the German citizens were approved and became law. For the Parliament to have reached this degree of agreement was by now an unexpected achievement. The Articles included equality before the law, freedom of worship and freedom of the press, freedom from arrest without warrant, and an end to discrimination because of class.

Apart from the constitution, other problems beset the Parliament. One concerned the territorial extent of 'Germany'. Should it include all the German-speaking lands, even those within that part of the Austrian Empire which lay outside the Confederation? The existing boundaries of the Confederation did not conform to any logical definition of 'Germany'. Parts of the Kingdom of Prussia and the Austrian Empire were included while others were not. Those parts that were within the Confederation contained many Czechs and Poles, while some of the excluded provinces had an overwhelmingly German-speaking population. The Austrian Empire, which comprised a host of different nationalities, was a major problem. Should all the Austrian Empire be admitted into the new Germany? Should only the German part of it be admitted? Or should none of it?

The Parliament was divided between the members who wanted a *Grossdeutschland* (Greater Germany), which would include the predominantly German-speaking provinces of the Austrian Empire, and those who favoured a *Kleindeutschland* (Little Germany), which would exclude Austria but include the whole of Prussia. The *Grossdeutschland* plan would maintain the leadership of Germany by Catholic Austria, while the *Kleindeutschland* plan would leave Protestant Prussia as the dominant German state. The Parliament was unable to decide between the two proposals – it did not seriously consider that the whole of Austria's Empire should be forced into a united Germany – and the argument dragged on inconclusively.

It had been an article of faith among most European liberals that all people would live in peace and harmony once they had thrown off the yoke of foreign oppression. The events of 1848–9 were to destroy these naive illusions. Relations between the peoples of central Europe deteriorated as national conflicts broke out between Magyars, Czechs, Croats, Poles, Italians and Germans. In general, the Frankfurt Parliament had little sympathy for non-Germans within Germany. Not wishing to see a diminution of German power, it opposed the claims of Poles, Czechs and Danes for territory seen as part of Germany, namely Posen, Bohemia and Schleswig-Holstein. (The Germans, it should be said, were no worse than other peoples in their attitude to minorities: Magyars, Czechs and Poles all demanded the inclusion of areas with large minorities.) Relations between Germans, Danes, Poles and Czechs deteriorated sharply.

From the start the Frankfurt Parliament lacked real muscle.

Unable to collect taxation, it had no financial power. Another problem worrying the Parliament involved the army. In order to exert its authority the central government would need a loyal army. The only army capable of acting as a national army in 1848 was the Prussian one. A Prussian general was appointed as Minister of War, but he agreed to accept the post only on condition that the Prussian army would remain independent. In addition, he insisted that he could not act in any way contrary to the wishes of the King of Prussia. As Minister of War he did try to persuade the rulers of Bavaria and Austria, the only states which had armies of any significance, to join with Prussia if 'exceptional circumstances' should make it necessary to field a national German army, but he failed. Without an army loyal to it, the authority of the central power remained theory rather than fact.

The Parliament was not in tune with the views of a large segment of the working class. German artisans established their own assemblies in 1848, the two most important meeting in Hamburg and Frankfurt. The Industrial Code put forward by the Artisan Congress in Frankfurt, as well as wanting to regulate hours of work and rates of pay, proposed to retain the restrictive practices of the old guild system. The Frankfurt delegates were mainly liberal. Regarding political freedom and economic freedom as inseparable principles, they rejected the Industrial Code out of hand. Many German workers thus lost faith in the Frankfurt Parliament.

Throughout the winter of 1848–9 the Parliament continued its debate, and in March 1849 a Constitution for a German Empire was finally agreed. There were to be two houses, the lower house to be elected by a secret ballot among men over the age of 25 and of 'good reputation', the upper house to be made up of representatives of the reigning monarchs and princes of the Confederation. The two houses would have control over legislation and finance, and although the Emperor would have considerable power, he would only be able to hold up legislation for a limited time. The Parliament, without much enthusiasm, offered the Crown to King Frederick William of Prussia.

3 The Revolution in Prussia

KEY ISSUE What were the main events in Prussia in 1848–9?

In 1848–9 the hopes of the Frankfurt Parliament lay with Prussia, and her King Frederick William IV. Frederick William was a strange and complex character, sensitive, cultured and charming, but moody and unstable. He was obsessed by a romantic and highly inaccurate vision of the Middle Ages, and looked back nostalgically to the days of the Holy Roman Empire. A fervent believer in the divine right of Kings, he had a mystical idea of kingship and its privileges and duties.

But he was far from a total reactionary. At the beginning of his reign, in 1840, it seemed that he might be a reforming monarch, who would make the government more liberal. But angered by opposition, Frederick William returned to restrictive policies. For most of the 1840s, he was a friend and ally of Metternich and dedicated to maintaining the old order in Europe. Then in 1847 he swung back to what at first seemed more liberal ideas and called a meeting of the United Diet in Berlin, which included representatives from all the provincial diets. Having called the Diet, the King made few concessions to its demands for liberal reforms and a written constitution. This uncertain wavering between the traditional conservative autocrat and the liberal monarch was a facet of his general instability and was a pattern which Frederick William was to repeat many times during the events of 1848–9.

When news of the February revolution in Paris reached Berlin, Frederick William's first reaction was to try to form a conservative front of states. Then on 13 March 1848 a demonstration by workers, mostly self-employed craftsmen, took place in the palace square in Berlin. The demonstrators threw stones at the troops and the troops replied by opening fire with cannon and rifles. Deputations of leading citizens now called on the King and asked him to make political concessions, while fighting continued in a confused way during the next two days. The original demonstrations, begun as a protest about pay and working conditions, quickly turned into a general, if vague, demand for 'the maintenance of the rights irrefutably belonging to the people of the state'.

On 16 March, news of revolution in Vienna and the dismissal of Metternich reached Berlin, and popular excitement rose even further. Frederick William accepted the idea of a new German constitution, agreed to recall the United Diet, and agreed to end censorship. On 18 March a large crowd collected outside the royal palace. The King appeared on the balcony and was loudly cheered. He then ordered the troops to clear the crowds, and shots were fired either in panic or by accident. Students and workers immediately set up barricades and serious fighting erupted. At least 300 rioters were killed as troops won control of the city.

The King, who all his life hated bloodshed and, most untypical for a Prussian, disliked the army and all military matters, decided to make a personal appeal for peace and calm. He wrote a letter 'To my dear Berliners' at 3 a.m. Copies were quickly printed and were put up on trees in the city centre early on the morning of Sunday, 19 March. It promised that the troops would be withdrawn if the street barricades were demolished. The concluding sentence read:

> Listen to the paternal voice of your King, you inhabitants of my true and beautiful Berlin; and forget the past, as I shall forget it, for the sake of that great future, which under the peace-giving blessing of God, is dawning upon Prussia, and through Prussia upon all Germany.

Troops were indeed withdrawn, largely due to a misunderstanding, so that the King was left in his palace guarded only by Berlin citizens who formed a Civic Guard. On 19 March he had little option but to appear on the balcony and salute the bodies of the dead rioters. Berliners hoped that Frederick William might become a constitutional monarch and that he might also support the German national revolution. On 21 March he appeared in the streets of Berlin with the German colours, black, red and gold, round his arm. Greeted with tumultuous applause, he declared: 'I want liberty: I will have unity in Germany'. In the following days he granted a series of general reforms, agreeing to the election of an assembly to draw up a new constitution for Prussia, and appointing a liberal ministry.

What were Frederick William's motives for this behaviour? Did he submit to the revolution from necessity, join it out of conviction, or, by putting himself at its head, try to take it over? Given his unstable character, he may well have been carried away by the emotion of the occasion and felt, at least for a short time, that he was indeed destined to be a popular monarch and national leader.

But the King's apparent liberalism did not last long. As soon as he had escaped from Berlin and rejoined his loyal army at Potsdam, he expressed very different feelings. He spoke of humiliation at the way he had been forced to make concessions to the people, no longer his 'dear Berliners', and made it clear that he had no wish to be a 'citizen' King. However, he took no immediate revenge on Berlin and allowed decision-making for a time to pass into the hands of the new liberal ministry. That ministry was hardly revolutionary. Its members were loyal to the crown and determined to oppose social revolution. Riots and demonstrations by workers were quickly brought under control by middle-class Civic Guard units. Meanwhile the ministry, supporting German claims to the Duchies of Schleswig-Holstein, declared war on Denmark. It also supervised elections to a Prussian Assembly on the basis of manhood suffrage. The new Assembly met in May. Although it was dominated by liberals, some 30 per cent of its members were radicals and there was no agreement about the nature of the new constitution. Its main achievement was to abolish the feudal and other legal and financial privileges of the Junker class.

Concerned at this radical action, Prussian landowners and nobles formed local associations to defend their interests. In August 1848 the League for the Protection of Landed Property met in Berlin. This '*Junker* Parliament', as it was dubbed by the radicals, pledged itself to work for the abolition of the Assembly and the dismissal of the liberal ministry.

In Potsdam Frederick William was surrounded by conservative advisers who urged him to win back power. The conservatives – Junkers, army officers and government officials – were not total reactionaries. Most hoped to modernise Prussia but insisted that reform should come from the King, not from the people. The tide seemed to be flowing in their favour. By the summer most Prussians seemed to have lost their ardour for revolution and for German unity. The liberal ministry was increasingly isolated. In August the King resumed control over foreign policy and concluded an armistice with the Danes, to the disgust of the Frankfurt Parliament. Riots by workers in Berlin in October ensured that the middle classes drew closer to the traditional ruling class. Habsburg success in Vienna in October also encouraged the King to put an end to the Prussian Assembly and to dismiss the liberal ministers.

In November 1848 Frederick William appointed his uncle Count Brandenburg to head a new ministry. Almost at once Brandenburg ordered the Prussian Assembly out of Berlin. The Civic Guard was dissolved and thousands of troops moved into Berlin. Martial law was proclaimed. All political clubs were closed and all demonstrations forbidden. There was little resistance to the counter-revolution. In provincial towns in the Rhineland and Silesia the army made short work of industrial unrest. The Assembly, still unable to agree a constitution, was dissolved by royal decree in December. Frederick William now proclaimed a constitution of his own.

The Prussian constitution of late 1848 was a strange mixture of liberal policies and absolutism. It guaranteed the Prussians freedom of religion, of assembly and of association, and provided for an independent judiciary. There was to be a representative assembly, with two houses. The upper house would be elected by older property-owners, and the lower one by manhood suffrage. The King could, however, in emergency suspend civil rights and collect taxes without reference to Parliament. Ministers were to be appointed and dismissed by the King, and were to be responsible only to him and not to Parliament. The King could alter the written constitution at any time it suited him to do so. He also retained control of the army. The constitution thus confirmed the King's divine right to rule whilst limiting his freedom to act in practice. A genuine parliament, albeit subservient to the crown, had been created – from above. While Frederick William would not accept limitation of his power imposed by any of his subjects, he was prepared to limit his own powers.

The new proposals were well received in Prussia, and ministers made no secret of the fact that they hoped it would be a better model for a united Germany than the Frankfurt Parliament. They had ambitions to make Prussia the leading state in Germany, and Frederick William the leading monarch. They hoped that Germany would be united not by a national Parliament, but by control imposed by Prussia.

4 The Failure of the German Revolutions

> **KEY ISSUE** Why did the revolutions fail?

a) The Failure of the Frankfurt Parliament

In the spring of 1849 the Frankfurt Parliament faced serious problems. By March 1849 the Habsburg Emperor Franz Joseph had regained control of all of the Austrian Empire except Hungary. Dissolving the Austrian Constituent Assembly, he subjected all parts of the Empire to rigid control from Vienna. In March Austria's chief minister Schwarzenberg proposed that the whole Habsburg domains, containing 38 million people, should be united with the German Confederation, containing 32 million people, forming a great empire of over 70 million people. This should be administered by a directory of seven, headed alternately by Austria and Prussia and assisted by a Chamber of Estates consisting of 38 Austrian ministers and 32 German.

Worse was to follow. In April 1849 Frederick William of Prussia refused to accept the crown of a united Germany. He would only accept it if the offer came from his fellow princes. He distrusted 'the gentlemen of Frankfurt' who had, he believed, taken it upon themselves to speak for a united Germany without any legal authority and was not prepared to be Emperor of Germany if it meant putting himself and Prussia under the control of the Frankfurt Parliament. Moreover, he was aware that if he accepted the crown from 'revolutionaries', this would have serious foreign policy implications and might even lead to war with Austria.

The rulers of Bavaria, Saxony and Hanover, together with Prussia, rejected the German constitution. Many members of Parliament now lost heart and, like the Austrian and Prussian representatives, went home. The remnants, about 130 of them, mostly from south German states, made a last attempt to recover the situation. They called for the election of the first new German Parliament, or *Reichstag*, in August. The call fell on deaf ears. The moment was past, the high hopes gone. The Parliament was driven out of Frankfurt by the city government and moved to Stuttgart, the capital of the Kingdom of Württemberg. There it was forcibly dispersed by the King's soldiers in June 1849. So ended the Frankfurt experiment.

b) Why Did the Frankfurt Parliament Fail?

The Frankfurt Parliament has been harshly treated, particularly by Marxist historians. Marx's friend Engels described it as 'an assembly of old women' and blamed it for not overthrowing the existing power structures. However, it is perhaps unfair to condemn the Parliament for failing to do something that it did not want to do. Most of its members had no wish to be violent revolutionaries and had little interest in social reform. Another charge levied against the Parliament is that its members were impractical idealists who wasted valuable time (six months!) discussing the fundamental rights of the German people. Unable to agree on a new constitution, it failed to grasp the opportunity of filling the power vacuum in Germany in 1848. In reality, however, there probably never was a real possibility of creating a unified German nation ruled by a German government in 1848–9. Had the members of the Frankfurt Parliament acted as decisively and quickly as their critics would have them act, they would probably have been dispersed far earlier than they were.

Austrian and Prussian attitudes were crucial. Constitutional government and national unity could only be achieved on their terms. Austria had no wish to see a more united or democratic Germany: she hoped to dominate Germany by keeping it weak and divided. The best, perhaps only, chance of the Frankfurt liberals lay in working out an agreement with Prussia. The chaos in Austria in 1848 gave Prussia a unique chance to play a dominant role in German affairs. She did not grasp this opportunity. This was a failure not just on the part of the King but also on the part of the Prussian liberal ministry. Both King and ministry failed because, in the final analysis, they were not at all anxious to succeed. King Frederick William, like most of his subjects, was unwilling to see Prussia merged in a united Germany at least in the way envisaged by the Frankfurt Parliament.

In fact, the authority of the Parliament was never accepted wholeheartedly by most of the individual states or their rulers. When the ruling princes feared that they were about to lose many of their powers or even their thrones because of revolutions within their territories, they were prepared to support the Parliament. By opposing it, they feared stirring up even more opposition. But once the rulers had re-established their authority, their enthusiasm waned. Attractive as might be the idea of a strong and united Germany in theory, in practice they had no wish to see their powers limited by liberal constitutions and a strong central authority.

When the new Austrian Emperor, Franz Joseph, regained control of all his territories in 1849, all hope of the Frankfurt Parliament experiment effectively ended. The Austrian government opposed all revolutionary change. And once effective Austrian opposition was established, it was almost certain that no other ruler would dare to be seen to be taking the lead in establishing a German Empire. By 1849 the Frankfurt Parliament, which had at first seemed to offer the way forward for national revival, became an irrelevancy and embarrassment. Most rulers were pleased to see it go.

There were other reasons for the Parliament's failure. One was the divisions among its members. The radical minority, who wanted to do away with the princes and replace them with a republic, found themselves in conflict with the majority of liberal members who wanted a moderate settlement which would safeguard both the rights of individual states and of the central government, and with a minimum of social change. There was also a small conservative group who wanted to preserve the rights of individual states and ensure that neither the Frankfurt Parliament nor the central government would exercise too much control. These groups were not organised like modern political parties, but were loose associations within which there were many shades of opinion and divergent belief. In addition to the three main groups there were a large number of independent, politically uncommitted members. For much of the time it proved impossible to resolve the differences between the members sufficiently to arrive at even a majority decision. This was something that the liberals, because of their numerical superiority, had not expected, and with which they were unable to deal successfully.

The Parliament was further handicapped by its unwise choice of leader, Heinrich von Gagern. He was a distinguished liberal politician, sincere and well meaning, but without the force of character needed to dominate the assembly and direct the debate.

Also, the Parliament lacked effective administration. No proper government organisation was set up, and the Parliament had no military backing to enforce its decrees. The Schleswig-Holstein episode showed its ineffectiveness. Denmark's decision to absorb the two provinces brought a noisy protest from Frankfurt. But not having an army of its own, it had to look to Prussia to defend German interests. Prussia did occupy the two duchies in April–May 1848 but King Frederick William, aware of Russian and British opposition and doubting the wisdom of war with Denmark agreed, in August, to the armistice of Malmo. The Frankfurt deputies regarded the Prussian withdrawal from Schleswig-Holstein as a betrayal of the German national cause but could do nothing about it.

c) Conservative Success

The failure of the Frankfurt Parliament was not quite the end of the 1848–9 revolutions. A wave of disorder swept through Germany in the spring and summer of 1849. Popular uprisings in Saxony, Baden, Bavaria and some Rhineland towns were put down by Prussian troops. Constitutional changes obtained from their rulers in Saxony, Hanover and several smaller states were revoked, and liberals all over Germany were arrested and imprisoned. Some were even executed. The lucky ones escaped into exile. In Prussia police powers were increased and local government powers reduced. The 'three-class suffrage' was introduced in elections for the Prussian lower house. The voters were divided into three classes each paying the same amount of tax and having the same amount of voting power. Thus a very small number of rich men in the first class had as much voting power as the bulk of the population voting in the third class.

By 1850 it seemed as if the events of the two previous years had never been; nothing had changed in most of the states. All traces of the Frankfurt Parliament were quickly cleared away. The black, red and gold 'flag of freedom' was removed from the hall of the Diet. The ships which the Parliament had bought as the nucleus of a national fleet were sold off at auction.

d) Why Did the Revolutions Fail?

By 1849 the hopes of the revolutionaries, so high across both Europe and Germany in the spring of 1848, had died. According to historian G.M. Trevelyan, 1848 was a potential 'turning point when Europe failed to turn'. By 1849 the forces of reaction were once again in the ascendant. The three dynastic empires of Austria, Prussia and Russia continued to dominate central and eastern Europe. No single new nation state had emerged. In 1851, as though to complete the restoration of old Europe, Metternich returned to Vienna to live as a revered 'elder statesman'. Most of the reasons for the failure of the German revolutions relate specifically to the situation in Germany. But the fact that revolutions failed across Europe in 1848-9 had an obvious impact on Germany.

In Germany active revolution was comparatively slight. In Prussia it was restricted to riots in Berlin and unrest in the Rhineland and Silesia. In most states there was little fighting and little bloodshed. In 1848 German rulers gave in easily, if temporarily, to demands for more democratic governments, fearing that otherwise they might be overthrown. The sensible course of action was to give way on easily reversed issues until the discontent subsided. But almost everywhere, they retained control of their armed forces and waited for an opportunity to regain power. Growing disunity among the revolutionaries gave them that opportunity.

There were wide differences in the political aims of liberals and radicals. While the former wanted constitutional government in all states and a united Empire with a national parliament, the latter worked for complete social and political change within a republican framework. Nor were the nationalists united in their specifications. There was little agreement on the form the new Germany should take – a unified state or a federation, a monarchy or republic, *Grossdeutschland or Kleindeutschland.*

Moreover, different social groups in Germany had very different interests. While popular movements were at the root of the revolutions, it was the propertied classes who seized power. Once middle-class liberals secured the election of their own assemblies, most were as afraid of social revolution as the conservatives. Working-class movements and the organisation of the radical left were not sufficiently well-developed to force social change in their favour. Most workers had a purely practical revolutionary aim: the removal of the intolerable pressures on their lives. Unlike their 'intellectual', usually self-appointed, leaders, they were not concerned with – or even aware of – political ideologies which supposedly espoused their cause. Nor were they united. Master craftsmen and the mass of unskilled workers had little in common. Karl Marx played only a minor role in the revolutions. Hastening back to Germany, like hundreds of other revolutionary exiles in 1848, he was disappointed by the apathy shown by the working class and correctly observed that the revolutions had staff officers and NCOs but no rank and file.

Germany was still essentially agrarian in 1848. The 1847 and 1848 harvests were reasonably good. Consequently, the rural populations were not generally in a desperate economic situation in 1848–9. This may explain the unenthusiastic support for revolutionary movements among peasants and their role in suppressing revolution by serving as loyal military conscripts. Across Germany, the peasantry lost interest in the revolution once the last remnants of feudalism had been removed. Indeed, many peasants felt hostility to, rather than affinity with, the urban revolutionaries. The failure of the peasantry to support the revolutions was of crucial importance.

Popular enthusiasms are often short lived and within a few months much of the active support for national unity and a national parliament had disappeared. This loss of support was encouraged by the slow progress being made by the Frankfurt Parliament. But, in general, national consciousness failed to affect the mass of Germans. Local loyalties and obedience to princely houses remained strong and proved an important obstacle in the way of national unity.

In the end the revolutions failed because the enemy was stronger, better organised and above all possessed military power. Constitutional government and national unity could only be achieved on the terms of the Princes, not through the well intentioned but ineffectual efforts of a liberal parliament, or by the uncoordinated actions of popular revolt. And it was clear in 1848 that attractive as the idea of a strong and united Germany might be in theoretical terms, the rulers felt that they had too much to lose by supporting the practicalities of unification offered by the Frankfurt Parliament. In any case, once order was restored in the Austrian Empire and the policy from Vienna was still based on dominating Germany by keeping her weak and divided, there was no possibility of any moves towards a more united Germany being allowed to take place. Germany would only be unified once the military might and moral authority of the Austrian Empire had been overcome.

e) Did the Revolutions Fail?

The failure of the 1848–9 revolutions was a severe setback for liberalism, not just in Germany but across Europe. However, the revolutions were not a total failure. At least the remnants of feudalism in Germany had been swept away. Parliamentary government of a sort had been introduced in Prussia. After 1848 virtually all the monarchical regimes in Germany accepted the need to modernise, even if most were still reluctant to accept a dilution of traditional forms of power. Conservatives also accepted the need to show an interest in the social problems of the lower classes if they were to win or maintain mass support for their policies and/or regimes. Moreover, the 1848–9 revolutions had probably helped stir national consciousness across Germany.

Summary Diagram
Germany in revolution, 1848–9

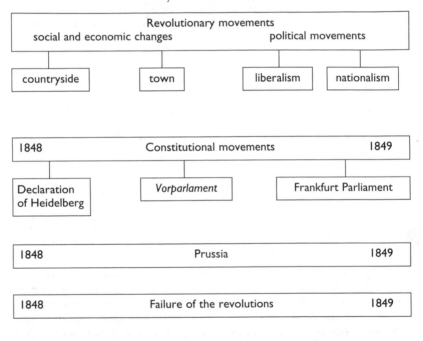

Working on Chapter 2

This chapter should give you an understanding of the causes of the revolutionary movements of 1848–9 and of the political and constitutional developments associated with them. You should have a framework on which to base a discussion of the reasons why, in the end, so little was achieved by the Frankfurt Parliament. You should also have some idea of what important events were taking place in Prussia in 1848–9 and why the Prussian revolution failed.

Answering structured and essay questions on Chapter 2

Consider the question:

Why did the Frankfurt Parliament fail to achieve its aims?

This is a straightforward 'Why' question. Construct an essay plan by going through the following three stages:

1. Make a list of statements which provide a direct answer to the question. Begin each with the word 'because'. For example, it failed 'because it was unrepresentative'.
2. List the facts you need to include for each statement to substantiate it.
3. Decide on an order of importance for your statements. Number them accordingly. Would you start with the most or least important. Why?

Another question on this period, for which it would also be well worth making an essay plan, is:

Why did the revolutionaries of 1848 achieve so little in Germany?

What would you include in an answer to this question that you have not included in the essay plan for the first question?

Source-based questions on Chapter 2

Source A: Frederick William's response to the offer of the German crown, made to him by a deputation of Frankfurt Parliament members in April 1849.

1 About the crown which the *Pauluskirche* has for sale; every German nobleman is a hundred times too good to accept such a diadem moulded out of the dirt and dregs of revolution, disloyalty and treason ... if accepted, it demands from me incalculable sacrifices and
5 burdens me with heavy duties. The German National Assembly has counted on me in all things, which were calculated to establish the unity, power and glory of Germany. I feel honoured by their confidence ... but I should not justify that confidence if I, violating sacred rights, were, without the voluntary assent of the crowned
10 princes and free states of our Fatherland, to take a resolution, which must be of decisive importance to them and to the states which they rule.

Source B: German cartoon: Panorama of Europe in August 1849

Source C: From *The Formation of the First German Nation-State,*
1800–1871, by John Breuilly, 1996

1 In fact, most energy [in Prussia] was devoted to internal problems
during 1848, following the collapse of crown authority in late March.
By November the king had regained the initiative and removed the
Prussian National Assembly from Berlin. In December he issued his
5 own constitution. In April he rejected the offer of the imperial
crown made to him by the German National Assembly. At the same
time he tried, both with governments and moderate nationalists, to
extend Prussian control over other parts of northern and central
Germany.

1. Study Source B.
    Explain the significance of the large figure with a broom in the centre of
    the cartoon? (*3 marks*)
2. Study Source A, B and C.
    To what extent do Sources A and B bear out the views expressed in
    Source C? Use your own knowledge to support your answer. (*7 marks*)
3. Study all three sources and use your own knowledge.
    Assess Prussia's role in the failure of the 1848–9 German revolutions.
    (*15 marks*)

3 Prussia and Austria 1849–66

POINTS TO CONSIDER

After the failure of the 1848–9 revolutions, it seemed that Austrian power had revived. Austrian policy was still based on dominating Germany by keeping it weak and divided. Germany would only be unified once the military might and moral authority of the Austrian Empire had been broken. The only country that could do that was Prussia. Historians are fond of describing the 1850s as a low point in the history of Prussia. At this time Prussia was regarded as the least important of the major Powers. But appearances were deceptive, for the foundations were being laid for the unification of Germany. In 1862 Otto von Bismarck was appointed Minister President of Prussia. Under his leadership Austria was defeated in the Seven Weeks' War of 1866 and the North German Confederation was established. How much of Prussia's success was due to Bismarck? How much was due to other factors?

KEY DATES

1850 Failure of Prussian Erfurt plan.
1851 German Confederation officially restored.
1861 William I became King of Prussia.
1862 Bismarck became chief minister.
1864 Austria and Prussia fought Denmark.
1866 Seven Weeks' War: North German Confederation set up.

1 Austrian Ascendancy

> **KEY ISSUE** Why did the Prussian Union Plan fail?

a) The Prussian Union Plan

Despite his refusal to accept the imperial crown offered by the Frankfurt Parliament, Prussian King Frederick William was attracted to the idea of a united Germany with himself at its head, providing he had the consent of the princes. In 1849 General von Radowitz, an ardent nationalist and monarchist and an old friend of Frederick William, came up with the Prussian Union Plan. His proposal for a *Kleindeutschland*, under Prussian leadership, met with Frederick William's approval. According to the plan, there would be a German Federal Reich (Empire), which would exclude Austria. It would have a strong central government and would give the King of Prussia control of the federal army. Although Austria would not be a member of the Reich, there would be a special relationship, a permanent 'union', between the Reich and the Habsburg Empire. This union would form a *Grossdeutschland* in which Austria and Prussia would be equal, but there would be no central government or any parliamentary assembly. The Reich itself would be based on the constitution drawn up by the Frankfurt Parliament, with Prussia as the leading state and the King of Prussia as Emperor.

This complicated plan, which tried to provide both *Kleindeutschland* and *Grossdeutschland* solutions, was not acceptable to Austria. Austrian chief minister Schwarzenberg saw it as a devious scheme to reduce Austrian influence in Germany. He was not, however, immediately able to mount effective opposition to it, as internal Austrian problems were occupying his attention. This allowed Prussia, whose army was the strongest authority in Germany in 1849, to press on with the plan. A 'Three Kings' Alliance' between Prussia, Saxony and Hanover was the first step. Then a number of smaller states were persuaded to fall in with the Prussian proposals. Encouraged by his success, Radowitz called a meeting of representatives of all the German states to Erfurt in March 1850 to inaugurate the new Reich. Representatives from 28 states agreed to the creation of the Prussian-dominated Erfurt Union. But several crucial states, suspicious of Prussian ambitions and fearful of Austria's reaction, declined to join. Schwarzenberg, having suppressed the Hungarian rising by August 1849, was now free to reassert Austria's position in Germany. He put forward a scheme of his own for a *Grossdeutschland* to be governed jointly by delegates from Austria, Prussia and the larger German states. Attracted by the way in which this proposal seemed to offer them greater political influence, some of the larger states such as Hanover and Saxony deserted Prussia and gave their support to Austria. Schwarzenberg was now able to summon the Diet of the old German Confederation, thought to have been dead and buried, to meet in Frankfurt in May 1850. The response was good and he was able to announce that the corpse had been revived and that the Diet and the Confederation were both alive and well. Thus by the summer of 1850 there were two assemblies claiming to speak for Germany: the Prussian-led Erfurt Parliament and the Austrian-led Frankfurt Diet.

A showdown soon occurred. In Hesse-Cassel, a member state of the Erfurt Union, a rising prompted its ruler to request help from the Frankfurt Diet. But the Erfurt Parliament also claimed the right to decide the dispute. Hesse-Cassel was of strategic importance to Prussia because it separated the main part of Prussia from the Prussian Rhineland, and therefore controlled communications between the two. The Prussian army mobilised, and Austria replied with an ultimatum that only the troops of the old Confederation had the right to intervene.

Small-scale fighting broke out between Prussian and

Confederation troops, but Manteuffel, the new Prussian Minister-President (Prime Minister), and his Minister of War had very little faith in their army and were anxious to avoid an all-out war.

A meeting between Manteuffel and Schwarzenberg was arranged at Olmütz and on 29 November 1850 Prussia agreed to abandon the Prussian Union Plan as it was clear that it was only supported by a minority of German states. Manteuffel and Schwarzenberg also agreed to a conference of states being held at Dresden early in 1851 to discuss the future of Germany. Schwarzenberg had won a major diplomatic victory. However, the revival of Austria was not allowed to go as far as he hoped. His proposal for an Austrian-dominated 'Middle Europe', incorporating 70 million people of all the German states and the Habsburg Empire, was not acceptable to the smaller German states, as it would have increased the power of the larger states at their expense. There was strong pressure for a return to the status quo of before the 1848 revolution and Prussia supported this at the conference. The Prussian Union Plan was lost, and anything was better than accepting the Austrian counterplan. In May 1851 the German Confederation of 1815 was formally re-established and an alliance between Austria and Prussia appeared to signal a return to the policy of close co-operation. Everything was as it had been: all signs of the events of the previous three years had been carefully covered over and consigned to decent obscurity.

However, the close co-operation which had characterised Austro-Prussian relations pre-1848 was now a thing of the past. Many Prussians blamed Austria for the humiliation of the 'Capitulation of Olmütz'. Some were determined that Prussia should one day dominate a united Germany. Austria clearly stood in the way. In 1856 an emerging Prussian statesman, Otto von Bismarck, commented:

> Germany is clearly too small for us both; ... In the not too distant future we shall have to fight for our existence against Austria ... it is not within our power to avoid that, since the course of events in Germany has no other solution.

b) Prussian Economic Success

Although Prussia had suffered a serious political setback, economically the story was very different. In the 1850s the Prussian economy began to boom. Industrial production, length of railway track and foreign trade more than doubled. The reasons for Prussia's success are complex. Scholars may have ascribed too much influence to the *Zollverein*. It did not provide protection for Prussian industries. Nor did it create a unified German economy. Other factors may have been equally or more important. Prussia had a good education system at various levels, from primary schools to university level. She possessed plentiful supplies of coal, iron and chemicals and had a good system of communications. A number of key individuals like Alfred Krupp, the great iron and steel magnate, played an important role. Historians disagree about the role played by the Prussian state. Some think it helped economic development. Others are convinced it hindered. For whatever reason, or more likely combination of reasons, by the mid-1850s, Prussia was economically stable and industrially expanding. In the struggle for the control of Germany, Prussia might have been too weak to tackle Austria on the battlefield, but economically her power, and therefore her ability to finance a full-scale war in the future, was increasing rapidly year by year.

In 1849 Austrian minister Schwarzenberg, realising the political implications of Prussia's economic success, proposed establishing a *Zollunion*, an extended customs union, between Austria and the *Zollverein*. This move failed. So too did Schwarzenberg's efforts in 1851 to establish an alternative customs union to include Austria and those German states still outside the *Zollverein*. Thus, while Austria clung to its political leadership of the Confederation, she was effectively isolated from the Prussian-dominated economic coalition of the German states.

Despite the development of railways, considerable industrial expansion and rapidly rising exports, the Austrian economy was in difficulties. Taxation was not sufficient to finance the newly reformed central administration, which became corrupt, nor to maintain the army, which became more and more inefficient. By the end of the Crimean War in 1856 Austria was economically and financially vulnerable, crippled by the cost of keeping her large armies mobilized during the war.

2 Prussia 1850–62

> **KEY ISSUE** What were the main developments in Prussia in the years 1850–62?

a) Conservative Reform

During the 1850s, Manteuffel showed himself to be a conservative reformer. He was prepared to accept limited change as long as it did not lead to any extension of parliamentary influence. He had a particular hatred of the liberal, educated, professional class, considering them to be arrogant, cowardly and godless. He believed the best way to stabilise society and reduce the chance of revolution was to improve the living conditions of peasants and workers.

He was especially concerned to help the peasants, because he believed that they were the basis of popular support for the monarchy. He persuaded Frederick William to free all the peasants from their traditional feudal obligations to their landlords. Special low interest government loans were available to enable peasants to buy their land, and 600,000 did so. In some parts of Prussia, where peasants had moved away to the towns looking for work, there was underpopulation in the countryside, but elsewhere there was overpopulation and great pressure on land. Where this was the case the government encouraged emigration, and gave peasants financial help to move to less populated areas of the country.

In towns the government set out to help factory workers. Payment of a standard minimum wage was strongly encouraged. Employers were no longer allowed to pay wages in overpriced goods instead of money. Financial help was given to industry, inspectors were appointed to improve working conditions in factories, and children under 12 were forbidden to do factory work. Industrial courts were set up to help in the settlement of industrial disputes.

In these ways Manteuffel aimed to unite the monarchy with its most underprivileged subjects. He believed that ministers had a duty to govern well, and that this meant governing in the best interests of all the people. If the ordinary people were happy and contented, the monarchy would not be undermined by liberals and socialists using social discontent to stir up trouble and possible revolution. At the same time he believed that ministers had a right to govern without reference to the people, and that there was therefore no need for representative assemblies of any kind. He governed without Parliament for the whole of his time as Minister-President (1850–8). In other ways he was equally reactionary, imposing strict censorship of the press and restrictions on the freedom of political parties to hold meetings. Prussia in the 1850s was thus a curious mixture, politically reactionary, socially reforming and economically prosperous.

b) The International Situation

Prussia seemed to be a second-rate power in the 1850s. Having avoided military conflict with Austria in 1850, she then played no role in the Crimean War. However, by remaining strictly neutral during the War, she benefited politically as well as economically. She managed to keep on good terms with the other Powers especially Russia. Austria also remained neutral. However, as a result of her wavering diplomacy, by 1856 she had lost the friendship of Russia without obtaining that of Britain and France. At one point in the war Austria had attempted to mobilise the forces of the German Confederation against Russia, but had been thwarted in the Diet by the Prussian representative, Bismarck.

Prussia might have profited from the north Italian war in 1859 (as Bismarck suggested) if she had supported Piedmont and France against Austria. However, popular feeling in Prussia, as in most German states, was anti-French. Prussia tried to benefit by offering Austria help in exchange for her conceding Prussia primacy in

Germany. Austria's speedy defeat and willingness to make peace with Napoleon prevented Prussia's aims being realised. But at least Austria's defeat was a severe blow to Austrian prestige.

c) William I

Frederick William, whose mental balance had always been precarious, became more and more unstable, until, in 1858, he was finally declared insane. His brother William became regent, and when Frederick William died in 1861, he succeeded to the throne as William I. William, already 63 when he became king, was to reign for another 27 years. A soldier by training and a conservative by instinct, William was practical, hardheaded and inflexible – the complete contrast to Frederick William. A devout Protestant, he believed that he was answerable only to God, which made it difficult to argue with him. He was prepared to listen to advice from ministers, but not necessarily to act on it. Only Bismarck, his chief minister for nearly the whole of his reign, was ever able to make him change his mind. At heart he was an absolutist, but he did believe in the rule of law. On becoming regent, he dismissed Manteuffel, replacing him with a ministry containing both liberals and conservatives. The atmosphere of comparative freedom led people to talk of a 'new era'. The 1858 elections gave the liberals a small majority in parliament. They hoped to play a significant role in government. William had no intention that they should.

d) Constitutional Crisis: 1860–2

As a soldier, the strengthening of the army was one of William's main concerns. He believed it was the key to the future greatness of Prussia. The mobilisation of the Prussian army during the war in Italy in 1859 between France and Austria had been a disaster. The army was in a state of confusion and quite unready to fight. Before it could be organised into some degree of order and readiness, the Austrians had been defeated and had made peace with France. The delay had lost William the opportunity to achieve some political advantage.

As a result of this ignominious failure, William appointed a new Minister of War, General von Roon. In 1860 Roon, an administrative genius and an extreme conservative, introduced a bill to reform and modernise the army. This aimed to double the regular army's size, increase the period of service from two to three years, reduce the role played by the inefficient, middle-class civilian militia (or *Landwehr*) and re-equip the troops.

Roon's bill touched a number of sensitive points as far as the liberal majority in Prussia's parliament was concerned. The bill greatly increased the military budget. The liberals feared that the government might use the expanded army, not for the defence of Prussia from foreign attack, but against its own people as had happened in 1848. Moreover, the civilian *Landwehr*, despite its military shortcomings, was popular with liberals. While there was some room for compromise on detail, both sides believed that important principles were at stake. William was determined that army matters should be kept above parliamentary approval. The liberals believed that parliament should have financial control over army expenditure. Without such a right it had very little power.

The army bill thus led to a constitutional crisis. In 1860 parliament would only agree to approve the increased military budget for one year and would not agree to extend the term of military service from two years to three. In June 1861 radical liberals formed the Progressive Party. The Progressives were committed to a popular rather than a royal army. In the newly elected parliament in December 1861, the Progressives won 110 seats and became the largest party. Parliament would not pass the money bill for the army and William would not accept the two-year military service. William again dissolved parliament and replaced his liberal ministers with conservatives. The May 1862 elections were a disaster for the King and a triumph for the Progressives, who in alliance with other opposition groups now had an overall majority in the lower house. In September parliament again refused to pass the army bill. William, fearing civil war in Prussia, contemplated abdication. However, on 22 September on the advice of Roon, he appointed Otto von Bismarck as chief minister. This was one of the great turning points in history.

3 Bismarck

> **KEY ISSUE** What were Bismarck's aims in 1862?

a) Bismarck's Background

Bismarck's father was a moderately wealthy *Junker*. The *Junkers* were the landowning nobility, with their own rules of conduct based on an elaborate code of honour, a strong devotion to the military life, a strong sense of service to the Prussian state and an even stronger sense of their own importance. Most were deeply conservative. Bismarck was proud of his *Junker* descent and all his life liked to present himself as a *Junker* squire, sometimes playing the part in a rather exaggerated way. He was often described as a 'typical *Junker*', which he was not. He was too clever, too enterprising, and too non-conformist for that.

Bismarck's mother came from a family of Hamburg merchants. Many of her relatives were civil servants, university professors or lawyers. Most were educated, intelligent and articulate, and politically

OTTO VON BISMARCK

1815 born, the son of a *Junker*: educated in Berlin and at Göttingen University. He developed a reputation as an accomplished duellist (in one year he fought 25 duels).

1836 left university with qualifications in law and entered the civil service.

1839 disliking civil service work, returned to manage family estates.

1847 married. Became an ultra-conservative deputy in the Prussian United Diet.

1851–9 served as Prussia's delegate at the Diet of the Confederation. He defended Prussian interests and became increasingly anti-Austrian.

1859 appointed Prussian ambassador to Russia.

1862 became Prussian special envoy in France: recalled to become Minister-President.

1864 War against Denmark.

1866 War against Austria.

1870–1 Franco-Prussian War.

1871–90 served as Chancellor of the new German Empire.

1898 died.

After 1862 Bismarck became a man of imperious and dominating temperament with an unquenchable thirst for power. He also saw himself as a man of destiny, convinced that he was destined for a great political role. However, he once admitted: 'I am all nerves; so much so that self-control has always been the greatest task of my life and still is'. He smoked 14 cigars a day, and said he hoped to smoke 10,000 before his death, as well as consuming drink and beer. He ate huge meals, and not surprisingly suffered from chronic indigestion for many years. In 1883 when his weight reached 114 kilos, he was put on a diet of herrings and eventually managed to lose 25 kilos. Given to melancholy, he suffered from periods of laziness. He was also an inveterate womaniser and gambler. Aggressive and emotional, his relations with William I were stormy; their meetings sometimes degenerated into slanging matches. Bismarck once pulled the handle off the door as he left the room, so great were his feelings of tension. Ruthless, vindictive and unscrupulous in getting his own way, he could also be charming and witty, a delightful companion and entertaining conversationalist.

liberal. Bismarck seems to have been ashamed of this side of his family, often speaking of them in a disparaging way, and comparing them unfavourably with his *Junker* ancestors. He did not get on well with his mother, who was livelier and cleverer than his father, but from her he inherited his intelligence, his quick wittedness and his determination.

At her insistence, he was sent away to school in Berlin, where he proved resistant to education, although he later became a good linguist, fluent in French, English and Russian. He was an excellent sportsman, being a good swimmer and rider, a crack shot and an expert fencer. He went on to Göttingen University, where he wasted a good deal of time and money, drank too much and got into debt. At the end of his first year he transferred to the University of Berlin, where he managed to pass his law examinations. This success won him entry to the Prussian Civil Service and Bismarck spent the next four years as a less than committed civil servant, eventually leaving his job, because he 'could not put up with superiors'. A reluctant year of military service followed, enjoyed neither by Bismarck nor the army. On his mother's death in 1839, he retired to help run the family estates. Country life soon bored him, and he found entertainment chasing after peasant girls and playing wild practical jokes on his neighbours.

By the time he was 30, in 1845, Bismarck had achieved little. His energies and abilities were being wasted. He was becoming bored and lazy, without purpose, when in 1847 two events occurred which changed the direction of his life. First he married and second he got involved in Prussian politics.

His wife Johanna von Puttkamer was a deeply religious Lutheran. 'I like piety in women and have a horror of female cleverness', he wrote. Johanna satisfied both his requirements. She persuaded Bismarck to become deeply religious himself. Providing a stable background to his life, she brought up their numerous children and overlooked his continued infidelities. When he fell in love with the wife of the Russian Ambassador, Johanna wrote, 'My soul has no room for jealousy and I rejoice greatly that my husband has found this charming woman'. Afterwards, as always, Johanna welcomed him back. She and the children remained an important part of his life, despite his later quarrels with his eldest son.

b) Bismarck's Political Career: 1847–62

In 1847 Bismarck was elected to the Prussian United Diet. It marked his entry into public life, but at the time no one, and certainly not Bismarck himself, could have foreseen the political career which lay ahead of him in the next 43 years.

During the March days of the Berlin riots in 1848, Bismarck involved himself in counter-revolutionary plots. He was a member of the right-wing *Junker* Party and excessively anti-liberal. 'Only two things matter for Prussia', he said, 'to avoid an alliance with democracy and to secure equality with Austria.'

In newspapers articles in 1850 Bismarck demanded equality with Austria in the Confederation, and in December of that year he spoke in the Erfurt Parliament in defence of Frederick William's 'surrender' to Austria at Olmütz. He argued that a state should fight only in its own interest – what he called 'state egoism' – and war for Hesse-Cassel would have been foolish.

> Gentlemen, show me an objective worth a war and I will go along with you ... woe to any statesman who fails to find a cause of war which will stand up to scrutiny once the fighting is over.

This speech gained promotion for Bismarck as Prussian envoy to the revived Diet of the Confederation at Frankfurt, where, apart from a short time in Vienna as Prussian ambassador, he remained until 1859. During his years at Frankfurt he gained a reputation for aggressive bad manners. It became his overriding concern in Frankfurt to counteract Austria's attempts to continue her leading role in Germany and to insist on Prussia's right to equality. He thus moved away from the views of his conservative Prussian associates who had sponsored his appointment to Frankfurt. They thought the fight against revolution was still the priority and that it required the solidarity of the conservative Powers Russia, Austria and Prussia. Not Bismarck. As a matter of course, he opposed most of Austria's proposals in the Diet. As he became increasingly anti-Austrian, he became convinced that war between Prussia and Austria was unavoidable. He argued that such a conflict would eventually lead to a divided Germany with a Protestant north and a Catholic south.

By 1858 he was arguing that Prussia should seek support among German nationalists and a year later that Austria should be driven out of the Confederation and a *Kleindeutschland* established under Prussian control. This was a theme he continued to develop over the next two years. By the early 1860s he had a reputation as a tough, able politician, ambitious and ruthless. Although viewed (mistakenly) as a conservative reactionary and (correctly) as a loyal supporter of the monarchy, he was also seen (with some justification) as an unconventional and unpredictable maverick.

c) What Were Bismarck's Aims in 1862?

Bismarck was to be the chief architect of the German Empire. In his memoirs, written in the 1890s, he depicted himself as a statesman who foresaw events and brilliantly achieved his goals. He left readers in no doubt that he was a veritable superman, working from the start of his political career for German unification. Some historians credit him with having a long-term strategy to make war on Austria and France in order to create a united Germany under Prussian control. As evidence, they cite the following words of Bismarck, allegedly spoken to Disraeli, a future British Prime Minister, in 1862:

1 As soon as the army shall have been brought into such a condition to
   command respect, then I will take the first opportunity to declare war
   with Austria, to burst asunder the German Confederation, bring the
   middle and smaller states into subjection and give Germany a national
5 union under the leadership of Prussia.

Other historians, like A.J.P. Taylor, are not convinced. They point out that the above quote was written down many years later by someone who was not present at the meeting. Taylor argued that Bismarck was merely an opportunist, essentially following his Lucky Star, cleverly exploiting his enemies' mistakes and taking calculated risks which happened to be successful. Bismarck himself said: 'one must always have two irons in the fire'. He often had many more than two. In consequence, it is difficult to disentangle with any certainty his aims, motives or the extent to which he planned ahead. Most historians think it unlikely that an unskilled statesman could have had so much luck. Nor is it likely that a skilled statesman had no plans. The general consensus is that Bismarck, at the very least, had a broad outline of what he wished to achieve in his mind from 1862. However, it is likely that he did not plan in any sense of mapping out a specific set of moves. He sought instead to reach his usually limited and clearly defined goals by taking advantage of situations that he either helped to create or that simply presented themselves to him.

Bismarck's main aim initially was Prussian domination of north Germany rather than full national unity. He was essentially a Prussian patriot rather than a German nationalist: his loyalty was to the Prussian King – not to the German people. Liberal nationalists viewed him with disfavour in the early 1860s, seeing him not as a potential unifier but as an anti-liberal reactionary. In the late 1840s and early 1850s Bismarck had shown little but contempt for nationalism, often referring in his letters to the 'nationality swindle'. However, by the late 1850s his views began to change. Aware of the popular appeal of German nationalism, he realised that the movement might be manipulated in the interests of enhancing Prussian power. Indeed, he tended to see Prussian and German interests as one and the same. He said in 1858 there was 'nothing more German than the development of Prussia's particular interests'. Convinced that great issues are decided by might not right, he was determined to make Prussia as mighty as possible. Prussian leadership in Germany would ensure Prussian might. While he was determined to end Austrian primacy in the Confederation, he was not committed to war to make this possible. A diplomatic solution, in his view, was a preferable option.

Realpolitik characterised Bismarck's career from first to last. The term is used to describe the realistic and often ruthless policies of politicians, like Bismarck, whose only aim was to increase the power of a state. While Bismarck was a sincere Protestant, he was able to divorce personal from political morality. What was good for Prussia was good. In his view, the end justified the means. He had contempt for idealism and idealists. His unscrupulous methods occasionally brought him into conflict with William I and the Prussian military and political elites. But while many distrusted his tactics, most respected his cool judgement and his flexible pragmatism and opportunism. Indispensable to the Prussian monarchy for nearly 30 years, he made the complex and difficult unification process appear, with hindsight, easy.

d) What Factors Helped Bismarck?

In 1869 Bismarck wrote:

> I am not so arrogant as to assume that the likes of us are able to make history. My task is to keep an eye on the currents of the latter and steer my ship in them as best I can.

He steered brilliantly. However, a variety of factors enabled him to bring about German unification.

i) The Prussian army

German unification was the immediate result of three short wars – against Denmark (1864), Austria (1866) and France (1870–1). The Prussian army thus made Germany a reality. The fighting capacity of the Prussian army improved immensely in the early 1860s thanks to the efforts and ability of War Minister Roon and General Helmuth von Moltke, chief of the General Staff. Roon ensured that Prussian forces were increased, better trained and well armed. Under Moltke, the General Staff became the brains of the Prussian army, laying plans for mobilisation and military operations. In particular, Prussian military chiefs were quick to see the potential of railways for the rapid movement of troops.

ii) Prussian economic success

Prussian economic growth in the 1850s and 1860s outstripped that of Austria and France. By the mid-1860s Prussia produced more coal and steel than France or Austria and had a more extensive railway network. In 1865 she possessed 15,000 steam engines with a total horsepower of 800,000. Austria, by contrast, had 3,400 steam engines with a total horsepower of 100,000. The economic and financial strength of Prussia gave her the military resources she needed to challenge first Austria and then France. A key industrialist was Alfred Krupp whose iron foundries in the Ruhr produced high-quality armaments.

iii) Economic unity and the Zollverein

The continued spread of the railway across many areas of Germany and the growth of an increasingly complex financial and commercial network helped draw together all parts of Germany into ever closer economic unity. So did the Prussian-dominated *Zollverein* which by 1864 included virtually every German state except Austria. However, while the *Zollverein* ensured that Prussia had considerable economic influence in Germany, this was not translated into political domination. Many German states supported Austria politically to counterbalance economic subordination to Prussia. In 1866 most *Zollverein* states actually allied with Austria against Prussia.

iv) German nationalism

The failure of the 1848 revolution was a serious blow to German nationalism. However, the idea of a unified state persisted in the hearts and minds of liberal-nationalists. In September 1859 the National Association was formed. Stimulated by the success of Italian nationalism in 1859, it promoted the idea that Prussia should lead the German cause (as the state of Piedmont had led the cause of Italian nationalism) and at the same time become more liberal in outlook. But gone was the romantic idealism of 1848. Many nationalists now accepted that nothing could be achieved without power. Only Prussia seemed to have that power. At its peak the National Association had only 25,000 members. It was banned in most of the main German states. However, it included many influential men who also had close links with a range of other organisations, not least with liberal parties which won growing support in many states, including Prussia, in the late 1850s and early 1860s.

There is no doubt that nationalist sentiment was strong among middle-class Germans who, as a result of industrialisation, were growing in economic and social power. The middle classes tended to lead public opinion. Books and newspapers supported the idea of national unity. There was an increased awareness of German culture – art, music, literature and history. A variety of national groups had large memberships. Moreover, fears of French expansion were still prevalent. Popular nationalism, strongest in the Protestant north, was a force that could not be ignored by Bismarck or any other ruler. However, there is plenty of evidence to suggest that the mass of Germans had little interest in national unity. The framework of most politicians in the early 1860s was local, not 'German'.

v) The international situation

The fact that Prussia was regarded as a second-rate power in 1862 helped Bismarck. He was able to achieve supremacy in Germany without arousing the hostility of Prussia's neighbours. In the 1860s Britain adopted a non-interventionist posture towards continental affairs. The prevailing view was that Britain had nothing to fear from

Protestant Prussia and that a strong Germany would be a useful bulwark against French or Russian expansion. Russia, concerned with reform at home, showed little interest in central Europe. Her sympathies lay with Prussia. She had still not forgiven Austria for her policy during the Crimean War and there was a growing clash of interests between the two in the Balkans. Austria's diplomatic isolation helped Bismarck. So did the fact that Austrian finances were in a perilous position. This meant that she was unable to modernise her army.

e) The Constitutional Crisis Solved

Bismarck's appointment as chief minister was seen as a deliberate affront to the Prussian liberals. They regarded him as a bigoted reactionary. Given that he had no ministerial experience, he was not expected to last long in power. On 30 September 1862, in his first speech to the Prussian Parliament, he declared:

1 Germany does not look to Prussia's liberalism, but to its power. Bavaria, Württemberg, Baden can indulge in liberalism, but no one will expect them to undertake Prussia's role ... It is not through speeches and majority decisions that the great questions of the day are decided.
5 That was the great mistake of 1848–9. It is by iron and blood.

This phrase, afterwards reversed to 'blood and iron', became almost synonymous with Bismarck. In truth, the speech was not his greatest effort. What he had meant to say was that if Prussia was to fulfil its role in leading Germany towards greater unity, it could not do so without an efficient army, which the King's government was seeking to build. His speech badly misfired. To most liberal nationalists such blood-curdling talk from a notorious reactionary was seen as a deliberate provocation. He thus failed to build any bridges to his political opponents.

In the end, he solved the problem of the military budget by withdrawing it, declaring that the support of parliament for the army bill was unnecessary as the army reforms could be financed from taxation. To liberal suggestions that the people should refuse to pay taxes, Bismarck replied that he had 200,000 soldiers ready to persuade them. Parliament declared his actions illegal but he ignored it. The taxes were collected and the army reorganised as if parliament did not exist. For four years and through two wars, he directed Prussian affairs without a constitutionally approved budgets and in the face of fierce parliamentary opposition. New elections in 1863 gave the liberals 70 per cent of the parliamentary seats. 'Men spat on the place where I trod in the streets', Bismarck wrote later. But he rightly judged that his opponents would avoid an appeal to force: indeed, they had no military force to pit against the King, who could also rely on the traditional support of his people. Bismarck also calculated that everything would be forgiven if he achieved foreign policy success.

4 Austro-Prussian Conflict

> **KEY ISSUE** Why did Austria and Prussia go to war?

a) Bismarck's Problems

Relations between Austria and Prussia, cool before 1862, became much cooler after Bismarck's appointment. In December 1862 he warned Austria that unless she recognised Prussia as an equal in Germany, she was inviting catastrophe. It should be said that in 1862–3 the prospect of Bismarck defeating Austria and bringing about a Prussian-dominated Germany was highly unlikely. Bismarck's own position in Prussia seemed vulnerable. Prussian (and German) liberals regarded him with hostility and contempt. In many respects Prussia's position in Germany was similarly vulnerable. Its territories straddled central Europe. Austria had a population almost twice that of Prussia and had a larger army. The majority of German states had no wish to be dominated by Prussia.

b) The Polish Revolt

A century earlier Prussia, Russia and Austria had divided Poland between them. Relations between Prussia and her Polish citizens had long been uneasy. Bismarck thought the Poles were troublemakers. In a private letter written to his sister in 1861 he advocated:

> Strike the Poles so that they despair for their lives. I have every sympathy for their plight, but if we want to survive we cannot but exterminate them.

In 1863 when the inhabitants of Russian Poland rose in revolt against the Tsar, Bismarck viewed the situation with concern. Trouble in any part of Poland could constitute a threat to Prussia as it could escalate into a general Polish uprising. The Tsar ordered the revolt to be suppressed. France, Austria and Britain protested and offered mediation. Bismarck took the opportunity to gain Russian friendship by sending an envoy to Moscow with offers of military assistance. The Tsar, confident he could defeat the Poles unaided, refused the offer but agreed to a Convention by which Prussia would hand over to the Russians any Polish rebels who crossed the border.

Prussian liberals, who hated autocratic Russia, protested at Bismarck's action. So too did France, Britain and Austria. Bismarck found himself isolated. In an attempt to extricate himself, he resorted to the pretence that the Convention did not exist because it had never been ratified. This angered the Tsar and Prussia was left completely friendless. The rising was finally suppressed in 1864. In the end Prussia emerged from the affair less disastrously than Bismarck deserved or expected. The Tsar had been offended by Austrian and French criticism, and, as a result, the danger of an Austrian-French-Russian coalition against Prussia, which Bismarck feared, now seemed even more improbable. It was far more likely that Prussia would be able to count on Russia remaining neutral in the event of war with Austria or France.

c) The Danish War: 1864

In November 1863 the childless King Frederick VII of Denmark died. Frederick had also been the ruler of the two duchies of Schleswig and Holstein which had been under Danish rule for 400 years. The population of Schleswig was mixed Danish and German, while that of Holstein was almost entirely German. Holstein was a member of the German Confederation; Schleswig was not. There had often been trouble over the Duchies. In 1848 the Holsteiners had rebelled against Denmark and Prussian troops had marched to their aid with the support of the Frankfurt Parliament, until Russian intervention had forced the Prussian army into retreat.

A treaty signed in London by the Great Powers in 1852 had agreed that Frederick would be succeeded as ruler of Denmark and of the Duchies by Christian of Glucksburg, who was heir to the Danish throne through marriage to the King's first cousin. Schleswig and Holstein contested his claim on the grounds that the Salic Law operated there. This law forbade inheritance through the female line, and the Schleswig-Holsteiners put forward their own claimant, the Prince of Augustenburg. He, however, did not object to being passed over in the treaty, having been well paid to agree, although he never formally renounced his rights.

When Christian became King of Denmark in November 1863, government officials in Holstein refused to swear allegiance to him and the son of the Prince of Augustenburg now claimed both duchies on the grounds that his father had never signed away his rights to them. This move was passionately supported by German nationalists. King Christian immediately put himself in the wrong by incorporating Schleswig into Denmark, thereby violating the 1852 Treaty of London. In December 1863 the smaller states of the German Confederation, condemning the Danish King's action as tyrannical, sent an army into Holstein on behalf of the Duke of Augustenburg, the Prince of Augustenburg's son. Augustenburg became the most popular figure in Germany, a symbol of nationalism, uniting both liberals and conservatives.

Bismarck was not influenced by German public opinion. However, he did see that the crisis offered splendid opportunities for Prussia. He hoped to annex the two duchies, strengthening Prussian power in north Germany and winning credit for himself into the bargain. He thus had no wish to see the Duke of Augustenburg in control of another independent state in north Germany. Nor did he care one iota about the rights of the Germans within the duchies. 'It is not a concern of ours', he said privately, 'whether the Germans of Holstein are happy'.

He first won Austrian help. Austrian ministers had very different aims from Bismarck. Austria, while supporting the Augustenburg claim, was suspicious of rampant German nationalism. Anxious to prevent Bismarck from allying Prussia with the forces of nationalism, she was happy to pursue her traditional policy of co-operating with Prussia. Bismarck, implying that he too supported Augustenburg, kept secret his own expansionist agenda. Agreeing to an alliance, the two Powers now issued an ultimatum to Denmark threatening to occupy Schleswig unless she withdrew the new constitution within 48 hours. Denmark refused. Thus, in January 1864 a combined Prussian and Austrian army, acting independently of the Confederation, advanced through Holstein and into Schleswig. Austria hoped she had taken Prussia prisoner. Bismarck was nearer the truth in his view that he had 'hired' Austria.

Failing to win the support of Britain, France or Russia, Denmark agreed that the Schleswig-Holstein matter should be resolved by the decision of a European conference. However, the London Conference (April–June 1864) failed to reach agreement. Counting on Britain's support, the Danes refused to make concessions and fighting recommenced. Despite British Prime Minister Palmerston's boast that 'if Denmark had to fight, she would not fight alone', there was little Britain could actually do – or did. Denmark quickly saw sense and surrendered in July 1864.

d) The Results of the Danish War

By the Treaty of Vienna in October 1864 the King of Denmark gave up his rights over Schleswig and Holstein which were to be jointly administered by Austria and Prussia. The question of the long-term fate of the Duchies soon became a source of acute tension between the two Powers, as Bismarck may have intended. Public opinion in Germany and the Duchies expected that Augustenburg would now become duke. However, Bismarck proposed that he be installed on conditions which would have left him under Prussia's power. This was totally unacceptable to Austria and to the Duke, who refused to become a Prussian puppet. Austria turned to the Diet. A motion calling for the recognition of the Duke of Augustenburg, easily passed. But Prussia, which had opposed the motion, ensured nothing was done. Thus by the summer of 1865 the future of the Duchies was still not settled, and tension between Austria and Prussia was high. Austria continued to support Augustenburg's claim while Prussia worked for annexation. 'We are reaching a parting of the ways', said Bismarck. 'Unfortunately our tickets are for different lines'.

But neither Austria nor Bismarck wanted war at this stage. Austria, almost financially bankrupt, regarded war as too expensive a luxury. Bismarck was aware that William I was reluctant to fight a fellow German state. Nor was he convinced that the Prussian army was yet ready to fight and win. While Bismarck and William I were 'taking the waters' at the fashionable Austrian spa town of Bad Gastein, an Austrian envoy arrived to open negotiations and to offer concessions over the Duchies. As a result of this meeting it was agreed in August 1865, by the Convention of Gastein, that the joint Austro-Prussian administration of the Duchies should be ended. The Duchy nearest to Prussia, Holstein, would be given to Austria and Schleswig, to Prussia to administer, but the two Powers would retain joint sovereignty over both Duchies. Bismarck knew he could now pick a quarrel with Austria over Holstein at any time he wanted.

Historians have argued for over a century about Bismarck's motives and about his aims in dealing with the Schleswig-Holstein affair. Had Bismarck used the Schleswig-Holstein crisis, as he later claimed, as a means of manoeuvring Austria into open confrontation with Prussia as a way of settling the problem of leadership in Germany? Or did he (whatever he said later) have no clear policy at the time except to 'allow events to ripen'? Historian A.J.P. Taylor thought that he 'may well have hoped to manoeuvre Austria out of the Duchies, perhaps even out of the headship of Germany, by diplomatic strokes ... His diplomacy in this period seems rather calculated to frighten Austria than to prepare for war'.

The particular problem of the Duchies was temporarily solved, but the more general problem of rivalry between Prussia and Austria remained. While Bismarck may not have wanted war at this stage, he realised that it was a distinct possibility. He thus did all he could to strengthen Prussia's international position. Confident that Britain and Russia were unlikely to interfere in a war between Austria and Prussia, his main fear was France. In October 1865 he met the French Emperor Napoleon III at Biarritz in the south of France. Historians continue to conjecture what occurred. Almost certainly nothing specific was agreed if only because neither man wanted a specific agreement. Bismarck was not prepared to offer German territory in the Rhineland in return for France's neutrality. Napoleon, calculating that a war between the two German Powers would be exhausting and inconclusive, intended to remain neutral and then to turn this to good advantage by mediating between the two combatants, gaining a much greater reward in the process than anything Bismarck could presently offer. Given Napoleon's anti-Austrian stance, it took little genius on Bismarck's part to secure the Emperor's good wishes.

e) War with Austria

Over the winter of 1865–6 Prussian–Austrian relations deteriorated. In February 1866 at a meeting of the Prussian Crown Council

Bismarck made a clear statement that war with Austria was only a matter of time. It would be fought not just to settle the final fate of the Duchies, but over the wider issue of who should control Germany. He would achieve by war what the liberals of 1848–9 had failed to achieve by peaceful means: a united Germany. But this united Germany would be under Prussian control.

The groundwork was carefully laid. A secret alliance was made with Italy in April 1866, by which Victor Emmanuel, King of Italy, agreed to follow Prussia if she declared war on Austria within three months. In return Italy would acquire Venetia from Austria as her reward when the war ended.

Immediately after the treaty with Italy had been signed, Bismarck stoked up tension with Austria over Holstein and over proposals to reform the Confederation. Bismarck knew that these proposals, which included setting up a representative assembly elected by universal manhood suffrage, would be unacceptable to Austria.

The Austrian army could not mobilise quickly, so the Austrians, afraid of a surprise attack, were forced to take what appeared to be the aggressive step of mobilising unilaterally in April 1866. Prussia mobilised in May, seemingly as a response to Austrian threats. Britain, France and Russia proposed a Congress to discuss the situation. Bismarck felt compelled to agree; to do otherwise would put him in a weak position. But he was very relieved when Austria refused, making the Congress unworkable. He kept up a front of wanting peace by sending an envoy to Vienna, but this mission came to nothing.

The situation deteriorated further when, in early June, Austria broke off talks with Prussia over Schleswig-Holstein and, and in breach of previous promises, referred the problem of the Duchies to the Diet. Bismarck's response was to send a Prussian army into Austrian-controlled Holstein. Austrian troops were permitted to withdraw peacefully. To Bismarck's surprise and disappointment this did not immediately lead to war. To stir things up, he presented to the Diet an extended version of his proposals for a reform of the Federal Constitution. Austria was to be excluded from the Confederation, there should be a national parliament elected by universal suffrage, and all troops in north Germany should be under Prussian command. The next day Austria asked the Diet to reject Prussia's proposals and to mobilise for war. Censored by the Diet, Prussia withdrew from the Confederation, declared it dissolved and invited all the other German states to ally themselves with her against Austria. Instead, most began mobilising against Prussia. Bismarck now issued an ultimatum to three northern states, Hanover, Hesse-Cassel and Saxony, to side with Prussia or else to be regarded as enemies. When the ultimatums were rejected, Prussian troops invaded the three states. Hesse-Cassel and Saxony offered no resistance, but Hanover fought until her army was defeated. The war had begun, without any formal declaration. Effectively a German civil war, it became known as the Seven Weeks' War, for that was the length of its duration.

The future of Bismarck, Prussia and Germany lay with the Prussian army. 'If we are beaten, I shall not return. I can die only once, and it befits the vanquished to die', said Bismarck, somewhat melodramatically. The Prussian army was under the command of General von Moltke, a gifted military leader. Advance planning and preparation, particularly in the use of the railways for moving troops, meant that mobilisation, while not perfect, was much more efficient than that of the Austrian army.

Austria's position was far from hopeless. She had more men, 400,000 to the Prussians 300,000, support from most of the other German states, and the advantage of a central position. Initially many Prussians were lukewarm about the war. In France the betting odds were four to one in Austria's favour. However, the Italians fulfilled their part of the secret treaty, following Prussia into the war. This meant that the Austrian army was forced to fight on two fronts, in the north against the Prussians and in the south against the Italians. The Italian army, weak and inefficient, was quickly defeated by the Austrians. To prevent the victorious Austrians in the south from linking up with their troops in the north, Moltke took the risk of crossing into Bohemia. One single-track railway ran from Vienna to Bohemia. By contrast Prussia used five lines to bring its troops southwards. Moltke adopted the risky strategy of dividing his forces for faster movement, only concentrating them on the eve of battle. Fortunately for Prussia, the Austrian high command missed several opportunities to annihilate the separate Prussian armies.

On 3 July 1866 the major battle of the war was fought at Sadowa (called Königgrätz by the Prussians). Nearly half a million men were involved, and the two sides were almost equally balanced. The Austrians were well equipped with artillery and used it effectively at the start of the battle, but they were soon caught in a Prussian pincer movement. The Prussians brought into use their new breech-loading needle guns. Its rate of fire was five times greater than anything the Austrians possessed, and it proved decisive. The Austrian army was forced to retreat in disorder. The Prussians had won the battle and with it the war because the Austrian government recognised that further fighting would almost certainly lead to further defeats and might even result in a break-up of the Empire. For Austria the priority was a rapid end to the fighting at any reasonable cost. Prussia was now in a position to dictate terms as the victor. It was a personal victory too for Bismarck, and put him in a position to dominate not only Prussia, but also the whole of Germany for the next quarter of a century.

Bismarck returned to Berlin with the King, Moltke and a hundred captured Austrian guns to a hero's welcome. A grateful Prussia, most of whose people had been no more than initially lukewarm about the war, presented him with a reward of £60,000, with which he bought a run-down estate at Varzin in Pomerania. He was promoted to Major General in honour of the victory. It had been noticeable that at meetings of the 'war cabinet' he had been the only one present wearing civilian clothes. Any uniform he was then entitled to would have marked him as an officer of lower rank than anyone else there, and he could not have borne that. Now he was a high-ranking officer he could flaunt his uniform on an equal footing, and he never again appeared in public except in full dress uniform. He had earned his spurs and intended to wear them in a Prussia, and later a Germany, dominated by military power.

After Sadowa, Austria was at the mercy of Prussia. William I had previously been unwilling to wage wholehearted war on a fellow monarch, but he now proposed an advance on Vienna. Bismarck, fearful that France and Russia might intervene and anxious to maintain Austria as a Great Power, counselled caution. He wrote to William as follows:

1   We have to avoid wounding Austria too severely; we have to avoid leaving behind in her unnecessary bitterness or feeling or desire for revenge. We ought to keep the possibility of becoming friends again. If Austria were severely injured, she would become the ally of France and of
5   every opponent of ours ... German Austria we could neither wholly nor partly make use of. The acquisition of provinces like Austrian Silesia and part of Bohemia could not strengthen the Prussian state; it would not lead to an amalgamation of German Austria with Prussia, and Vienna could not be governed by Berlin as a mere dependency.

At a noisy and angry meeting of the 'war cabinet' on 23 July, William I and his senior generals raged against Bismarck's policy of not annexing any Austrian territory, while Bismarck himself was in a state of nervous collapse and floods of tears in an adjoining room, threatening suicide if his advice was not taken. In the end Bismarck got his way. The war was brought to a speedy end and a moderate peace concluded with Austria. The only territory lost by Austria as a result of the Seven Weeks' War (Holstein apart) was Venetia in Italy. Ironically, Austria had won substantial victories against Italian forces, both on land and at sea.

ACTIVITY

Read carefully the extract from Bismarck's letter to William I in 1866. Answer the following questions:
a) Bismarck gives two major reasons for not annexing Austrian territory. What are they?
b) What evidence does the extract contain about Bismarck's interpretation of the phrase 'German nationalism'?
c) Bismarck often expressed contradictory views on the same topic. This means that his statements must be corroborated with other evidence as far as possible. Is it likely that Bismarck genuinely held the views expressed in the letter? Explain your answer.

5 Prussian Ascendancy

> **KEY ISSUE** What were the results of the Seven Weeks' War?

a) The Treaty of Prague

An armistice was signed between Prussia and Austria in July and was followed by a peace treaty, the Treaty of Prague, in August. The terms of the treaty were mainly concerned with the remodelling of North Germany as Prussia wished. Prussia annexed a good deal of territory, including both Schleswig and Holstein, as well as Hesse-Cassel, Hanover, Nassau and Frankfurt, along with their four million inhabitants. All other German states north of the River Main, including Saxony, were to be formed into a North German Confederation under Prussian leadership (see map on page 71).

Bismarck might have pressed for the unification of all Germany in 1866. However, as well as the threat of French intervention, he also feared that if Prussia absorbed too much too soon, especially the anti-Prussian Catholic south, this might be more trouble than it was worth. The four states south of the River Main – Bavaria, Württemberg, Baden and Hesse-Darmstadt – thus retained their independence. But all agreed to sign a secret military alliance with Prussia, whereby, in the event of war, they would not only fight alongside Prussia but would put their armies under the command of the King of Prussia. Why the states agreed to sacrifice their military sovereignty so readily is not certain. Perhaps they were sufficiently afraid of Bismarck to feel safer in some sort of alliance with him. They also feared a possible French attack.

The treaty of Prague is usually seen as a milestone on the way to German unity. Ironically in 1866, by destroying the unity of the German Confederation, it could be seen as dividing rather than uniting Germany. After 1866 Germans were separated into three distinct units: the North German Confederation; the four South German states; and the Austrian Empire.

b) The North German Confederation

Bismarck had shown a calculated moderation and clemency in his treatment of Austria. He showed neither of these to his fellow north Germans. Hesse-Cassel, Nassau, Hanover, Frankfurt and Schleswig-Holstein were not consulted about uniting with Prussia; they were just annexed. The wealthy city of Frankfurt had not opposed Prussia during the war, but was taken over just the same. The city was starved into surrender and was fined the enormous sum of 25 million guilders, with one million guilders interest for every day the fine remained unpaid. The burgomaster hanged himself. The aged King

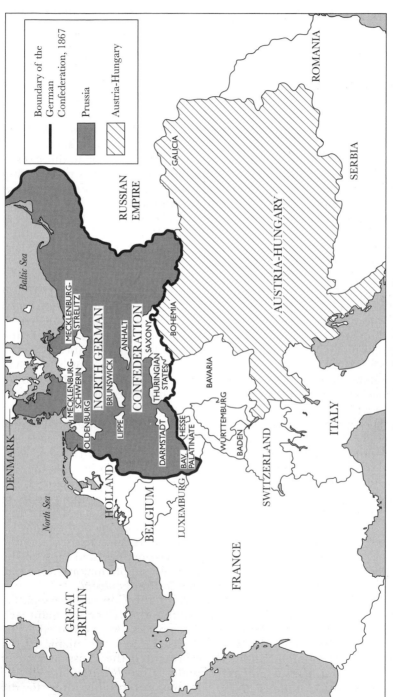

Germany and Austria in 1867

of Hanover was driven out, his personal fortune confiscated (it came in useful to Bismarck later when it was used to bribe the King of Bavaria), and his kingdom taken over by Prussia.

Those north German states, such as Saxony, not annexed by Prussia were left with some independence within the North German Confederation. Some historians have seen this as a trial run by Bismarck for an eventual wider federation taking in all *Kleindeutschland*. They argue that as he had no scruples he could easily have annexed the remaining northern states if he had so wished and did not do so because he wanted to show the Germans south of the Main not only how considerate an ally Prussia could be to those states which co-operated with her, but also how advantageous membership of a Prussian-controlled federation could be. This argument does not seem very convincing. More credible is the suggestion that he saw no advantage to Prussia in too speedy a takeover of so many states at once. Such action would only lead to a dilution of Prussian culture and traditions. Instead of Prussia absorbing Germany, Germany would end up absorbing Prussia.

At the end of 1866 Bismarck began drafting the constitution for the North German Confederation. This was accepted in April 1867 and came into effect in July 1867. The North German Confederation lasted only four years, but its constitution was to continue, largely unaltered, as the constitution of the German Empire. It was designed to fit the requirements of Prussian power and Bismarck's own political position.

The King of Prussia was President of the North German Confederation and also the commander-in-chief, and had the power of declaring war and making peace. He appointed and could dismiss the Federal Chancellor.

The states, including of course Prussia, had substantial rights, keeping their own rulers and being governed by their own laws and constitutions with their own parliamentary assemblies. They had their own legal and administrative systems, and local taxation met the cost of government services, provided education and supported the Church. The *Bundesrat* (the Federal Council) was the upper house of the Confederation's parliament. Here the various states were represented by delegates who acted on the instructions of their governments. The number of delegates was fixed in relation to the size of the state: out of 43 votes, Prussia had 17, Saxony four and most of the others one each. Decisions were made by a simple majority vote and, in practice, Prussia was never outvoted in the *Bundesrat*.

The *Reichstag* was the lower house of the Confederacy's parliament. It was elected by universal manhood suffrage – a giant step towards democracy. However, its powers were limited. The Federal Chancellor (the Chief Minister) was the main driving force in the Confederation. He represented the Prussian king in the *Bundesrat*. He was not responsible to the *Reichstag* nor did he need majority support in it. He was responsible only to the

President of the Confederation, who could appoint or dismiss the Chancellor.

All laws needed approval of the *Reichstag*, the *Bundesrat* and the King of Prussia as President of the Confederation. They also needed the signature of the Chancellor.

Bismarck was always opposed to the idea of parliamentary government on the British model, which reduced the crown to symbolic status and put power in the hands of parliament. His declared view of the political abilities of his fellow Germans was very low:

> Considering the political incapacity of the average German, the parliamentary system would lead to conditions such as had prevailed in 1848, that is to say weakness and incompetence at the top and ever new demands from below.

Given his views, Bismarck's insistence on universal manhood suffrage in the election of the *Reichstag* is somewhat surprising. However, he believed that the traditional loyalties of peasants would preserve the conservative order in Germany (as they did in France) and thus had no problem with the concept of universal suffrage. However, he did not intend the *Reichstag* to be much more than an organ of public opinion – a political safety valve playing an insignificant part in public life. Speaking in confidence to a Saxon minister, he declared he was trying 'to destroy parliamentarianism by parliamentarianism'. In effect, he hoped that the activities of a weak *Reichstag* would help to discredit parliamentary institutions in German eyes. Certainly, the democratic manner of the election did not compensate for the great weakness of the *Reichstag*, that ministers, including the Chancellor, were not members of it and were not responsible to it.

c) Popular Support for Bismarck

On the same day as the Battle of Sadowa, elections were held in Prussia. Patriotic war fever resulted in a big increase in the number of conservatives elected to the Prussian Parliament. The numbers jumped from 34 to 142, while the liberal parties were reduced from 253 to 148. Moreover, after news of the victory and after the terms of the peace treaty were announced many liberals changed their attitude to Bismarck. He was now acclaimed rather than maligned. This ensured an era of harmony between Bismarck and the Prussian parliament. Only seven votes were cast against an Indemnity Bill introduced by Bismarck at the beginning of the new session. This Bill asked Parliament to grant an 'Indemnity' for any actions taken by the government during the previous four years without Parliament's consent. Bismarck appealed for better relations between Parliament and the government and spoke of the need for the government to work jointly with Parliament to build a new Germany.

Both the left- and right-wing parties in Parliament split into new groupings. A large section of the old Liberal Party formed themselves into the National Liberal Party, pledged to support Bismarck in his nationalist policy, but equally pledged to maintain liberal constitutional principles against any government attempt to undermine them. Miquel, co-founder of the National Association and now a National Liberal leader, expressed the party's basic philosophy:

> The time for idealism is over. German unification has descended from the realm of speculation to the prosaic world of reality. Today politicians should be much less concerned than ever before with what is desirable in politics as opposed to what is attainable.

On the right, the Junker Party opposed Bismarck as a revolutionary and a traitor to his class, whittling away at the royal prerogative and losing Prussia's identity in the new unified North Germany. Moderate conservatives formed a new party group, the Free Conservatives. They, together with the National Liberals, were to provide the support which Bismarck needed to carry out his policies.

The first *Reichstag* was elected in February 1867. The National Liberals were the largest single party in it and held the balance of power between Bismarck's conservative supporters and his various opponents. They were able to win a number of concessions from Bismarck, now the Federal Chancellor. These included a secret instead of an open ballot at elections, and the right to pass an annual budget. This financial control was very limited because it did not include control over the military budget, which accounted for about 90 per cent of the Confederation's spending. The Liberals and Bismarck struggled over the question of the military budget and eventually reached a compromise. It would remain outside the *Reichstag's* control until 1872. Then the amount of money to be spent on the army would be fixed by law and for this the *Reichstag's* consent would be required. Generally prepared to support Bismarck's policies, the *Reichstag* carried through an ambitious legislative programme including a range of unifying measures.

d) Bismarck and Germany

The Treaty of Prague brought huge gains to Prussia. Austria was now forced to withdraw from German affairs, leaving the field clear for Prussia to dominate. Two-thirds of all Germans, excluding German Austrians, were now part of the Prussian-dominated North German Confederation. Most north Germans quickly accepted the situation. For many liberal-nationalists there was no irreconcilable differences between Bismarck's Prussian policy and *Kleindeutsch* nationalism. Unification was happening, even if it was being carried out by force, and some Liberals accepted that the end justified the means. Indeed, after 1866 Bismarck found himself under nationalist pressure, north and south, to complete the process of unification.

Recognising that union with the southern states would strengthen Prussia in relation to both France and Austria, Bismarck was not averse to the idea and was prepared to use the rhetoric and emotion of German nationalism to help bring it about.

In 1866 the tide in south Germany in favour of union with the North seemed to be flowing strongly. Political parties were established in the southern states to work for unity. In 1867 the four southern states were incorporated into the new *Zollparlament* – a parliament elected to discuss the policy of the *Zollverein*. This was intended to encourage closer cooperation between north and south. However, by 1867 local loyalties in the south re-emerged. Many southern Catholics regarded Prussia with suspicion and sympathised more with Austria. The foreign minister of Baden described the North German Confederation as a 'union of a dog with its fleas'. In 1868 the southern states elected a majority of delegates (49 to 35) to the *Zollparliament* opposed to union with the north. Bismarck was not too concerned. He believed that in good time, whether by war or simply as a result of evolution, the southern states would fall like ripe fruit into Prussia's basket.

Working on Chapter 3

Your notes on this chapter should make clear the changing relationship between Prussia and Austria in the period 1849 to 1866, during which the balance of power was reversed. Austria was supreme in 1849–50 after the failure of the revolutions and of the Erfurt Parliament. In the 1850s there was growing political and economic rivalry between the two powers. In 1862 Bismarck was appointed Minister-President of Prussia. Under his leadership Austria was totally defeated in the Seven Weeks' War of 1866, and the North German Confederation was established.

Answering structured and essay questions on Chapter 3

It is likely that evidence from this chapter will be needed to answer a general question on the unification of Germany discussed on pages 96 and 97. However, you may also find yourself facing a question specifically on the relationship between Prussia and Austria. For example:

Why had Prussia, rather than Austria, achieved dominance in Germany by 1866?

This is a straightforward 'Why' question. The temptation is to draw up a chronological list of points, beginning with Austrian superiority, moving on to the rivalry of the 1850s and ending with the Prussian victory of 1866. Unless you are careful the danger is that you will end up writing a narrative essay rather than an analytical one. It is better to look for another way of grouping your points which is not based on chronology. One obvious possibility is by broad aspects, such as military, economic and political.

Plan an answer to the question using these three broad aspects. Under each one, list the points you would make. Then decide what evidence you would include to substantiate each point. In what order would you consider the broad aspects? Why?

Source-based questions on Chapter 3

Source A: From *The Formation of the First German Nation-State, 1800–70* by John Breuilly (1996)

1   Many historians have exaggerated the extent of Bismarck's achieve-
    ments in laying the groundwork for the war against Austria. Britain and
    Russia were always unlikely to intervene; Italy was anxious to use the
    Austro-Prussian conflict to secure Venice. ... Indeed, one could argue
5   that any ordinary statesman in Berlin bent on war with Austria would
    not have done significantly worse.

Source B: From *The Fontana History of Germany 1780–1918: The Long Nineteenth Century* by David Blackbourn (1997)

1   There was no Bismarckian 'master-plan', only the firm determination to
    secure Prussia's position in north Germany and maintain the substance
    of the military monarchy. At the great-power level, Bismarck pressed
    for advantage when he saw it, but the chief characteristics of his policy
5   were flexibility and the skilful exploitation of opportunities. He always
    tried to keep alternative strategies in play – in his own metaphor, to use
    every square on the chessboard. Within that broad framework,
    Bismarck's policy towards Austria, for all its tactical twists and turns,
    was more single-mindedly bent on a particular outcome than his policy
10 towards France or the southern states.

Source C: Some statistical comparisons

	Population (million)		Relative share of world manufacturing output		Key outputs in 1870	
	1840	1870	1830	1860	Coal	Steel
PRUSSIA GERMANY	14.9	19.4				
	32.6	40.8	3.5	4.9	23.3	0.13
AUSTRIA-HUNGARY	30 [est.]	34.8	3.2	4.2	6.3	0.02

	Austria		France		Prussia	
Military						
1850	434,000		439,000		131,000	
1860	306,000		608,000		201,000	
1866	275,000		458,000		214,000[a]	
1870	252,000		452,000		319,000[b]	
Education	Primary	Secondary	Primary	Secondary	Primary[e]	Secondary
1850[c]	2,413,000	48,000	3,322,000	47,900	2,583,565	103,863
1865[d]	2,654,000	80,600	4,437,000	65,700	2,825,322	90,899
Railways (kilometres in operation)						
1850	1,579		2,915		5,856[f]	
1860	4,543		9,167		11,089	
1870	9,589		15,544		18,876	

[a] In 1866 Italy, Prussia's ally, had an army of 233,000.
[b] By 1871 the German States under Prussia's leadership could mobilise 850,000 men.
[c] The dates are actually 1851 for France, 1854 for Austria and 1852 for Prussia.
[d] The dates are actually 1865 for Austria and France, and 1864 for Prussia.
[e] Prussian figures exclude private schools.
[f] The figures are for the territory of the 1871 *Reich*.

1. Study Source C. How does this source help to explain Bismarck's policy towards Austria? (*3 marks*)
2. Study Sources A and B.
   With reference to your own knowledge explain the difference in emphasis between the two sources. (*7 marks*)
3. Study Sources A, B and C and use your own knowledge.
   Why was Prussia able to defeat Austria in 1866? (*15 marks*)

4 Prussia and France 1862–71

POINTS TO CONSIDER

In 1870 Emperor Napoleon III declared war on Prussia. The Franco-Prussian War was to have huge results for Germany, France and Europe. 'The war represents the German revolution', said British statesman Disraeli, 'a greater political event than the French Revolution of last century ... There is not a diplomatic tradition which has not been swept away ... The balance of power has been entirely destroyed'. Who or what was responsible for the war? Why did the Prussians win?

KEY DATES

1867	The Luxemburg Crisis.
1868–70	The Hohenzollern Candidature Crisis.
1870 July	The Ems telegram.
	Start of Franco-Prussian War.
September	Napoleon III surrendered at Sedan.
1871 January	German Second Empire proclaimed at Versailles.
January	France accepted an armistice.
May	Treaty of Frankfurt.

1 Franco-Prussian Relations: 1866–70

> **KEY ISSUE** Why did Franco-Prussian relations deteriorate?

a) Relations between Napoleon and Bismarck pre-1866

Bismarck had visited Paris for the World Fair in 1855 and while there had met the Emperor Napoleon III. This first meeting was a successful one on a personal level, and the two men parted on friendly terms. Their paths were to cross throughout the 1860s in very varied circumstances, and their final meeting – to discuss the French surrender in 1870 – took place in a very different atmosphere from the first.

Nephew of Napoleon I, Louis Napoleon had a hectic and colourful early career. He was involved in revolutionary activities, belonged to secret societies, was imprisoned, escaped, plotted and intrigued throughout Europe. In 1848 he was elected President of the French Republic, but overthrew it in 1852 and made himself Emperor of France as Napoleon III at the age of 44, when his health was already beginning to fail.

The motives behind Napoleon III's foreign policy are somewhat difficult to determine. He seems to have wanted simply to restore France to a position of influence in Europe, through peaceful means if possible. But the difficulty he had in making a decision and sticking to it made him appear inconsistent and unpredictable. Unlike his uncle, Napoleon I, he lacked the ruthlessness and the will to carry things through to their logical conclusion.

This put him at a marked disadvantage when dealing with a man as devious and determined as Bismarck, who was likely to outplay him at his own game. Yet the logic of the international situation in the early 1860s suggested that the two men could act in close association with one another. Both wanted to overturn the territorial arrangements made at Vienna in 1815 and there was sufficient 'available' land for both to make gains. Therefore Bismarck soon turned to France as Prussia's obvious ally of the future.

In 1865 Bismarck began to search for allies in a possible war with Austria. To sound out Napoleon's feelings, Bismarck went to his second meeting with the Emperor, this time at Biarritz, in October 1865. The exact details of the conversation are unknown. Bismarck's own version is sketchy and vague and is little help. Historians have speculated ever since on what passed between them. Maybe Bismarck made a deal with Napoleon by agreeing on territorial or other rewards for French neutrality in the event of an Austria-Prussian war, but it is unlikely that Bismarck, with his preference for keeping his options open, would have committed himself so far in advance. More probably he suggested vaguely that an opportunity might arise for French expansion, perhaps in the Rhineland, after a Prussian victory over Austria. Almost certainly there was no commitment on either side, but there probably were protestations of good will and general support. After all, Bismarck had remarked earlier in the year that 'Prussia and France are the two states in Europe whose interests make them most mutually dependent'.

However, Bismarck had some doubts about Napoleon's intentions and was not certain that he could rely on his protestations of neutrality. He was right, for Napoleon was sending supportive messages to Vienna as well as to Berlin. He was hedging his bets, by keeping on good terms with both Prussia and Austria and at the same time pursuing his own goals. He hoped to be able to turn his neutrality to good advantage by mediating between the combatants and by threatening to join in the war to persuade them to make peace on his terms, which would include territorial gains for France.

The speed and scale of Prussia's victory in the Seven Weeks' War (see pages 68–9) made it impossible for Napoleon to carry through his intentions. When he attempted to mediate after the Battle of Sadowa, the offer was declined by Bismarck, who instead sent the Prussian ambassador in Paris to inform Napoleon that Prussian expansion would be limited to north Germany, and that the south

German states would remain independent. This planned division of Germany was presented to Napoleon as a reward for his neutrality during the war because Bismarck realised that Napoleon would regard a united Germany as a potential threat to France. Bismarck explained in his *Reminiscences,* written nearly 30 years later, that he felt it necessary to appease Napoleon and leave Germany divided, because he thought that Napoleon was about to join a coalition with Austria against Prussia. For the same reason, he claimed, he made sure that Austria was generously treated in the peace settlement, as this would make it less likely that Austria would seek revenge in the future by allying herself with France, or 'any other enemy' of Prussia. Most historians doubt that Bismarck had the situation as carefully thought out as this at the time.

The Treaty of Prague was signed on 23 August 1866 and confirmed for Napoleon that he would not face a united Germany north and south of the River Main. The south German states had been guaranteed an 'independent international position'. However, the guarantees were not worth the paper they were written on, for Bismarck had made military alliances with the south German states even before the treaty was signed (see page 70).

Soon afterwards Bismarck extended the *Zollverein* to include the four southern states and involved them in the new *Zollparlament,* or customs parliament. Although it was nominally concerned only with economic affairs, Bismarck hoped that the *Zollparlament,* as a Prussian dominated institution, would in due course turn its attention to non-commercial business as well. It would be a further step in the Prussian domination of Germany.

Even if Bismarck had not planned to unite Germany north and south of the River Main, it is highly probable that it would eventually have come about, whatever Napoleon wanted. The North German Confederation represented more than two-thirds of Germany, now that Austria had been excluded, and it was unrealistic to suppose that the remaining third could or would continue an independent existence.

The four south German states did not present a united front, for they distrusted each other as much as they distrusted Bismarck. In addition they distrusted Napoleon with good reason. In July 1866 the French ambassador in Berlin had presented detailed plans to Bismarck for France to acquire part of the Rhineland belonging to Bavaria and Hesse. This would restore the French frontier to the 1814 line.

The idea was firmly rejected by Bismarck who did not want to give away any German territory to France. But nor did he want to alienate Napoleon. He therefore suggested that France should look for compensation, not in the German-speaking Rhineland, but further north in the French-speaking areas of Belgium and Luxemburg.

b) The Luxemburg Crisis

Having missed the chance to check Prussia's growth of power in 1866, Napoleon needed a diplomatic and territorial success to prove that France remained Europe's greatest power. Luxemburg seemed Napoleon's best bet for a showy success.

Bismarck's policy on the Luxemburg question is difficult to unravel. He began by helping Napoleon to 'persuade' the King of the Netherlands, who was also Duke of Luxemburg, to relinquish the Duchy. The King readily agreed. However, Prussia also had certain rights in Luxemburg, in particular to garrison the fortress. This right dated from the Vienna Settlement of 1815, which had made the fortress part of the German Confederation.

But by the end of 1866 Bismarck was feeling much less need to be friendly towards Napoleon, who was stirring up demonstrations in Luxemburg against 'the hated domination of Prussia' as part of his campaign in the Duchy. This created much anti-French feeling in Germany. Partly in response to this and partly to encourage national-ist feelings Bismarck now began to refer to Luxemburg as German, and announced that its surrender to France would be 'a humiliating injury to German national feelings'. He denied any responsibility by Prussia for the agreement between Holland and France. Invoking German nationalism, he declared: 'If a nation feels its honour has been violated, it has in fact been violated and appropriate action must ensue. ... We must in my opinion risk war rather than yield.' Anti-French sentiment continued to increase throughout Germany.

Why did Bismarck encourage this nationalist hysteria? It seems unlikely that he wished to start a war with France at this stage. He did not believe that the Prussian army was as yet strong enough, and he knew that the North German Confederation was still fragile. His intention perhaps was to start a campaign of provocation to drive Napoleon into war in due course or perhaps he now realised that he was in a strong enough diplomatic position to stop France making any territorial gains. In a long interview which Bismarck gave to a British journalist in September 1867 he spoke of his wish for peace:

1 There is nothing in our attitude to annoy or alarm France. ... there is
   nothing to prevent the maintenance of peace for ten or fifteen years, by
   which time the French will have become accustomed to German unity,
   and will consequently have ceased to care about it.
5 I told our generals this spring, when they endeavoured to prove to me,
   by all sorts of arguments that we must beat the French if we went to
   war then, 'I will still do all I can to prevent war; for you must remember, gentlemen, a war between such near neighbours and old enemies
   as France and Prussia, however it may turn out, is only the first of at
10 least six; and supposing we gained all six, what should we have succeeded in doing? Why, in ruining France certainly, and most likely ourselves into the bargain. Do you think a poor, bankrupt, starving, ragged

neighbour is as desirable as a wealthy, solvent, fat, well clothed one? France buys largely from us, and sells us a great many things we want.
15 Is it in our interest to ruin her completely?' I strove for peace then, and I will do so as long as maybe; only, remember German susceptibilities must be respected, or I cannot answer for the people – not even for the King!

In this interview Bismarck presented himself as a man of peace. He wanted to allay British fears about Prussian warlike intentions and to reduce the chance of a British alliance with France. He made use of methods like this interview with a respected foreign journalist to present himself and his policies in a favourable light to those whom he wished to influence. He understood very well the use of propaganda and the value of a good public relations system. This makes it difficult to arrive at the truth about his intentions from his public utterances. He did not always believe what he said, or say what he believed.

While Bismarck was declaiming his pacific intentions and playing down the danger of war, Napoleon III was under attack at home. He needed to raise his prestige and unwisely proclaimed that only his intervention had halted the Prussian advance on Vienna after the Battle of Sadowa. Bismarck took umbrage at the implications that his actions were controlled by Napoleon, and in March 1867 he released texts of the secret military alliances he had made with the South German states before the Treaty of Prague. These showed that the North German Confederation and the states to the south of the River Main were not as independent of each other as had been assumed.

Napoleon and Bismarck now met head on in a series of diplomatic battles. Napoleon began new negotiations with the King of the Netherlands. The King agreed to sell Luxemburg for 5 million guilders, subject to approval by the King of Prussia! This, he must have known, was not likely to be given. Indeed, Bismarck used the patriotic German fervour he had encouraged as an excuse to threaten the King of the Netherlands not to give up Luxemburg, and Napoleon lost any chance he might have had of acquiring the Duchy.

Bismarck appealed to the Great Powers to settle the question. A conference was held in London at which Luxemburg was declared neutral, under a collective guarantee. The terms of the guarantee were not very strong, but they did keep the French out of Luxemburg. As part of the agreement, the Prussian garrison was withdrawn. While the outcome of the London conference seemed like a compromise, the fact that there was no territorial gain for France was a heavy blow for Napoleon.

The Luxemburg crisis seriously damaged Franco-German relations. Nevertheless, the years 1867–70 were peaceful. Bismarck was still keen to avert war. Fearful of French military strength, he was also concerned that Napoleon might find allies. Austrian Emperor Franz Joseph, hankering after regaining influence in Germany, twice met Napoleon in 1867 to see if it was possible to reach agreement. Fortunately for Bismarck, these efforts came to nothing. There was no real basis for agreement. Franz Joseph was aware that most German Austrians totally opposed a pro-French and anti-Prussian policy.

The Luxemburg crisis has been described by some historians as the point at which Bismarck stopped being a Prussian patriot and became a German one. There is no evidence that Bismarck himself thought this. He stirred up and used German national feelings quite cynically as a means to increase Prussian influence over the rest of the German states, as well as a weapon against France. He was, however, aware that without some external intervention the unification of Germany under Prussia was unlikely to happen overnight. He spoke of 25 years as a probable time-scale.

When he floated his new idea in 1870 that the King of Prussia should take the title of Kaiser (or Emperor) of Germany, it was turned down by the rulers of the other German states. The *Zollverein* and *Zollparlament* had done valuable work for economic unity, but political unity was as far off as ever.

Some historians believe that Bismarck had come to the opinion that, whatever he might say in public to the contrary, a full-scale foreign war was needed to raise national consciousness and bring the people together. As if on cue the Hohenzollern candidature crisis developed.

2 War with France

> **KEY ISSUE** Who was most to blame for the Franco-Prussian War?

a) The Hohenzollern Candidature Crisis

In 1868 the Queen of Spain, Isabella, was driven out of the country by a revolution. The Spanish government made efforts to find a new monarch among the royal houses of Europe. An approach was eventually made to Prince Leopold of Hohenzollern. The senior branch of his family was the Prussian royal house. Bismarck always claimed that he had nothing to do with the matter until the crisis broke in July 1870, and that before then it was entirely a Hohenzollern family affair. Yet as early as May 1869, when there were rumours that the throne was being offered to Prince Leopold, Bismarck was involved in denying them.

In February 1870 an official offer was made to Leopold by the Spanish government. His father referred the request to William I who, as King of Prussia, was head of the Hohenzollern family. William left to himself would have refused consent. He knew that to proceed would provoke French hostility, for Napoleon would see it as a threat to 'encircle' France, with Hohenzollern monarchs in Berlin and

Madrid pursuing anti-French policies simultaneously. William was persuaded to change his mind by Bismarck, who sent him a strongly worded memorandum: 'It is in Germany's political interest that the house of Hohenzollern should gain in esteem and an exalted position in the world'. In the end the King gave his consent, provided that Leopold himself wished to accept the throne. As Leopold did not want to do so, the affair appeared to be at an end.

But Bismarck had secretly sent envoys to Spain, accompanied by large sums of money as bribes to push Leopold's candidacy. He also put pressure on the Hohenzollern family, as a result of which Leopold decided to accept after all. In June William, although annoyed at these underhand dealings, gave his unconditional consent.

Bismarck had planned that the document giving Leopold's acceptance would arrive in Spain, be immediately presented to the Cortes, the Spanish Parliament, for ratification, and then the news be announced amid general rejoicing. But the message relayed through the Prussian embassy in Madrid suffered an unforeseen mix-up of dates due to a cipher clerk's error. As a result the Cortes was not in session when the document arrived and before it could be recalled the secret of Leopold's acceptance leaked out.

The news reached Paris on 3 July. Napoleon and his new aggressive foreign minister Gramont regarded Leopold's candidature as totally unacceptable. An angry telegram was sent to Berlin asking whether the Prussian government had known of Leopold's candidacy and declaring that 'the interests and honour of France are now in peril'. Count Benedetti, the French ambassador in Berlin, was instructed to go to the spa town at Ems, where William I was taking the waters, to put the French case that Leopold's candidacy was a danger to France and to the European balance of power, and to advise William to stop Leopold leaving for Spain if he wanted to avoid war.

William was distressed by events and assured the ambassador of Prussia's friendship for France, for the last thing he wanted to see was war over Leopold. On 12 July Leopold's father withdrew his son's candidacy. Once again the affair appeared to have been settled, with the diplomatic honours going to France. Bismarck, in Berlin, spoke of humiliation, and threatened resignation. In the nick of time he was saved from having to make good his threat.

Napoleon, goaded by the Empress Eugenie and foreign minister Gramont, now overplayed his hand. Leopold's renunciation had been announced in a telegram from his father to the Spanish government. Now the French demanded an official renunciation from William I, on behalf of Leopold, for all time, and the French ambassador was ordered to see the King again and obtain his personal assurance. They met on 13 July. William refused to give the assurances demanded since he had already given his word. Even so, his reply was conciliatory. As a matter of course he instructed one of his aides to

notify Bismarck, in Berlin, of the day's events in a telegram. He also
gave him permission to communicate details to the press.

b) The Ems Telegram

That evening, in Berlin, Bismarck, dining with Generals Moltke and
Roon, received the telegram from Ems (see page 96). Having read it,
Bismarck, 'in the presence of my two guests, reduced the telegram by
striking out words, but without adding or altering anything'. The
shortening of the text of the telegram had the effect of making the
King's message to the French ambassador appear to be his immediate
and uncompromising response to the French demand to renounce
support for the Hohenzollern candidature for all time. Bismarck in
his *Memoirs*, written in the 1890s, describe his actions as follows:

1 The difference in the effect of the abbreviated text of the Ems telegram
   as compared with that produced by the original was not the result of
   stronger words, but of the form, which made this announcement
   appear decisive, while the original version would only have been
5 regarded as a fragment of a negotiation still pending and to be continued at Berlin. After I had read out the concentrated version to my
   two guests, Moltke remarked. 'Now it has a different ring. In its original
   form it sounded like a parley; now it is like a flourish in answer to a challenge'. I went on to explain: 'If in execution of His Majesty's order, I at
10 once communicate this text, which contains no alteration or addition
   to the telegram, not only to the newspapers but by telegraph to all our
   embassies it will be known in Paris before midnight ... and will have the
   effect of a red rag on the French bull. Fight we must if we do not want
   to act the part of the vanquished without a battle. Success, however,
15 depends essentially upon the impression which the origination of the
   war makes upon us and others: it is important that we should be the
   ones attacked'.

Bismarck personally handed the amended text of the Ems telegram to
the newspapers for publication in a special edition in Berlin and sent
it for publication abroad. By morning the news was on the streets of
Paris. The alterations had made the King's actions seem more abrupt
and dismissive than they really were, and when William saw the published version he is said to have remarked with a shudder, 'This is war'.

It seems probable that Bismarck had had in mind since 1866 an
eventual war against France, as long as it could appear to be a defensive war, brought about by French aggression. Such a war would serve
as nothing else could to bring the south German states into the
Prussian fold. He was well aware that war is a great national unifier.
All that was needed was a suitable opportunity. This occurred with the
Hohenzollern candidature crisis, and Bismarck took full advantage of
it. However, there is little evidence that he was set on war from 1866
or even in 1870. Nor did he control the whole Hohenzollern affair

from 1868 to 1870. What he did do was to manipulate and take advantage of the situation. But it was not simply opportunism on his part which led to war. Equally important were a series of French diplomatic blunders. Moreover, the French Emperor and people in 1870 were ready to fight. If Bismarck set a trap for France, it was largely one of France's own making.

As Bismarck had anticipated, the publication of the amended Ems telegram caused eruptions in France. French newspapers and crowds, convinced that French honour was at stake, demanded war. Napoleon, urged on by his wife, his ministers, the Chamber of Deputies and public opinion, declared war on Prussia on 19 July. Bismarck, claiming that France was the aggressor who had 'committed a grievous sin against humanity', called upon the south German states for support in accordance with the terms of their military alliances with Prussia. Convinced that the Fatherland was in danger, they agreed to support Prussia.

c) The Franco-Prussian War

European historians are not in agreement about what to call the war – should it be Franco-Prussian (the usually accepted name) or Franco-German? In different ways it was both. It was the first genuinely German war, fought by the newly defined *Kleindeutschland,* but it was so dominated by Prussian expertise that it was little more than an extended Prussian military enterprise. Bismarck and Moltke organised the German war effort and Prussian troops outnumbered all other troops in the army. But all the German states fought under Prussia, presenting a united front, even if at the beginning some support was less than enthusiastic.

By the end of the war this had changed, and all Germany was united by a blind hatred of France and all things French. This was brought about by government propaganda, and particularly by Bismarck's inflammatory speeches, letters and newspaper articles. This enmity remained after the peace treaty as one of the permanent legacies of the war.

It was a war with only two combatant nations: Germany and France. Russia had promised to fight alongside Prussia if Austria joined France – this was enough to keep both Russia and Austria neutral. Denmark toyed with the idea of supporting France in the hope of recovering Schleswig from Prussia, but in the end did nothing, while Italy made such outrageous demands on France as the price of her support that Napoleon would not accept them. Britain was not prepared to intervene in a war that did not appear to affect her interests. Long mistrustful of Napoleon's ambitions, she was certainly unwilling to come to France's assistance, particularly after Bismarck made it appear as if the French Emperor was about to invade Belgium in defiance of the long-standing British guarantee of Belgian independ-

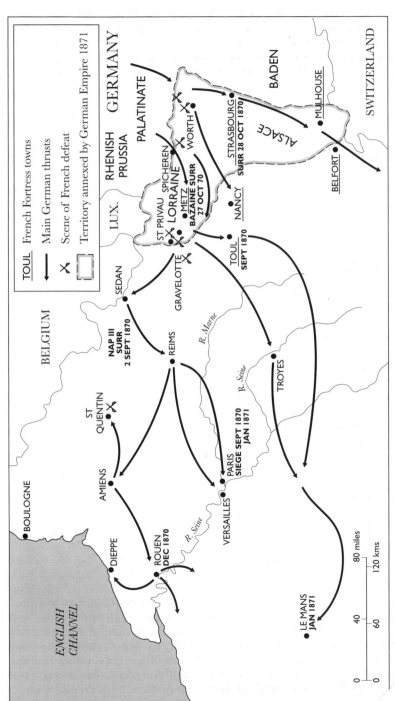

Map of the Franco-Prussian War

ence. He did this by publishing in *The Times* an undated version of draft documents given to him by the French ambassador in 1867, when they were discussing possible 'compensation' for French neutrality during the Seven Weeks' War. These documents mentioned Belgium specifically, and Bismarck appears to have kept them carefully for use in just such circumstances as arose in July 1870.

The Prussian army, with troops from the other German states, was quickly mobilised. Mobilisation had been well planned, and nearly half a million troops had been moved by train into the Rhineland, on the borders of Alsace, by the beginning of August. There were six German railway lines to the French frontier: the French had only two. The German soldiers were generally well trained, and they were under the command of the brilliant General von Moltke. French mobilisation was slower and not complete by the time Napoleon III arrived at Metz to take supreme command.

The first battles of the war took place at the beginning of August. Moltke's grand strategy was initially bungled by the mistakes of his field commanders. French troops, armed with the *chassepot* rifle, which was superior to the Prussian needle gun, and with elementary machine guns, the *mitrailleuses,* fought well in the first battles. However, the fire power of the Prussian Krupp breech-loading artillery proved decisive.

These early German victories had a catastrophic effect on Napoleon and Marshall Bazaine. They went on the defensive, withdrawing 180,000 men into the fortress of Metz. There would be no French invasion of Germany. The only question was how long it would be before a German invasion of France began. It came a week later on 14 August, when the German armies crossed the River Moselle at several points and advanced beyond Metz to cut off the French escape route to Paris. Two days later the French army in Metz attempted to withdraw to the north, but was defeated in a fierce battle and forced to retreat into the fortress again. There it remained besieged until it finally surrendered at the end of October. The decision to remain in Metz was fatal to the French cause for it meant that the bulk of Napoleon's finest troops were out of action.

Napoleon had left Metz when the fighting began and reached the River Marne, where a new French army was hurriedly collected together under the command of MacMahon. MacMahon set off with 130,000 men to find and rescue the army which was supposed to be breaking out of Metz in the direction of Sedan. The German army intercepted MacMahon's forces and drove them back in confusion towards Sedan. On 1 September the most important battle of the war began, watched from a hill top by William I, Moltke, Bismarck and a selection of German princes. The French commander refused to consider a retreat despite the severe battering his troops were receiving from the 600 German guns surrounding Sedan. Napoleon rode round during the battle, looking hopefully for a bullet or shell which

Napoleon III and Bismarck after Sedan

would spare him the disgrace of surrender. He did not find one. That night Bismarck, Moltke and the French commander met to discuss surrender terms. In a letter to his wife Bismarck described what happened next:

> 1 Yesterday at five o'clock in the morning, after I had been discussing until one o'clock in the morning with Moltke and the French generals the terms of the capitulation, General Reille woke me to tell me that Napoleon wished to speak with me. I rode without washing and with no
> 5 breakfast towards Sedan, and found the Emperor in an open carriage, with six officers, on the high road near Sedan. I dismounted, greeted him as politely as if we were in the Palace of the Tuileries in Paris and asked what were His Majesty's commands. On Napoleon's asking where he should go, I offered him my quarters at Donchéry near Sedan.
> 10 ... Before we reached the place he began to be apprehensive that we might meet a number of people, and asked whether we could stop at a lonely labourer's cottage by the road. It was miserable and dirty, but 'No matter' said Napoleon; and I ascended with him a narrow rickety staircase. In a room three metres square, with a deal table and two rush
> 15 bottomed chairs, we sat an hour while the others remained below – a contrast to our last interview. ... We sent out one of the officers to reconnoitre and he discovered a little villa a kilometre away in Frenois. There I accompanied the Emperor and there we concluded with the French General the capitulation, according to which forty to sixty thou-
> 20 sand French – I cannot be more accurate at this time – with all that they had, became our prisoners. The day before yesterday and yesterday [1 and 2 September 1870] cost France one hundred thousand men and an emperor. ... This has been an event of vast historic importance.

ACTIVITY

Read carefully the extract from Bismarck's letter to his wife and study the illustration on page 89. Answer the following questions:

a) What conclusions can be drawn from Bismarck's evidence about Napoleon's state of mind? Support your answer with evidence.

b) What, apart from providing a factual account of what happened, appear to have been Bismarck's motives in writing his letter? Support your answer with evidence.

c) The painting was not an attempt to make a visual record of what actually happened. It was painted with other purposes in mind. Using evidence from the painting, suggest what these other purposes might have been.

d) In what ways do the letter and the painting i) support and ii) contradict each other?

Thus ended the final meeting between Bismarck and Napoleon in a situation which neither of them could have foreseen in 1855 when they met in Paris.

The day after the battle, under the terms of surrender agreed in the early morning, the Germans took prisoner 84,000 men, 2,700 officers, 39 generals and one emperor. Later additions brought the total number of prisoners to over 104,000. Napoleon was taken to Cassel, where he remained until the spring of 1872, before going into exile in England, where he died the following year. When the news of the defeat and of the Emperor's capture reached Paris on 4 September, he was deposed by a revolutionary government. The Second Empire was abolished and the Third French Republic was proclaimed in its place.

The war should by rights have finished at this point. There were few French troops available to continue the fighting, for most of them had either surrendered at Sedan or were still besieged in Metz. Little stood in the way of a German advance on Paris. To everyone's surprise the war was to last for another six months. German forces surrounded Paris by the middle of September, and settled down to starve the city into surrender. The government of the new French Republic struggled to raise an army to relieve the siege of Paris. Although there was no difficulty in finding soldiers for the army, it was impossible to find enough trained men to act as officers. The result was a large, undisciplined, enthusiastically patriotic mob, which proved no match for the experienced German army. By January 1871 Parisians, desperately short of food, were also subject to bombardment by German guns. On 28 January 1871 the French government finally agreed to accept an armistice.

3 The Results of the War

> **KEY ISSUE** What were the main results of the war?

a) The German Empire

From the start of the war Bismarck had determined that King William I of Prussia should become Emperor of Germany. This was not an easy matter. The four southern states had to accept him. Moreover, William himself was reluctant to accept a 'German' title, which would take precedence over his Prussian one. He was also determined that the offer of the Imperial crown should come from the Princes, not from the German people, as it had done in 1849. In October 1870 Bismarck began his complex negotiations.

He was helped by the fact that the successful war against France created a tidal wave of German patriotism. Popular pressure in the four southern states for turning the wartime alliance into a permanent union grew. This strengthened Bismarck's negotiating hand with the south German rulers. Seeking to preserve Prussian influence at the same time as creating a united Germany, he was determined that the new Reich would have a constitution similar to that of the North German Confederation. The south German rulers, by contrast, wanted a looser system in which they retained more rights. Bismarck had to use all his diplomatic skill to get his way. His trump card was the threat to call on the German people to remove those rulers who stood in the way of unity. He also made some symbolic concessions, most of which meant little in practice. King Ludwig II of Bavaria, who was particularly reluctant to co-operate, was finally won over by a secret bribe: Bismarck agreed to pay him a large pension to pay off his debts. (He used the money confiscated from the King of Hanover in 1866.)

In November 1870 separate treaties were signed with each of the four south German states by which they agreed to join the German Empire. The new Reich was a federal state: constituent states retained their monarchies and had extensive power over internal matters. But real political power was in the hands of the Emperor, his army officers and his hand-picked ministers of whom Bismarck, the new Imperial Chancellor, would be chief.

Ludwig II, King of Bavaria agreed to put his name to a letter asking William to accept the title of Emperor. The other princes were then persuaded to add their names, and the document was sent to William. The appeal was seconded in December 1870 by a deputation to William from the North German *Reichstag*. Strangely enough the President of the *Reichstag* in 1870 was the same man who had been spokesman for the Frankfurt Assembly when it offered the imperial crown to Frederick William in 1849. This time, though, the Parliament had only a subsidiary role to play and was merely a backing group for the Princes.

On 18 January 1871 King William I of Prussia was proclaimed Kaiser, or German Emperor, not in Berlin but in the French palace of Versailles just outside Paris. Soon after midday the King of Prussia entered the Hall. A short religious service was held, enlivened by a fiery sermon directed against the French. After a brief speech of welcome by the King, Bismarck, in splendid array in his pale blue military uniform, stepped forward to read the proclamation:

1 We William, by the Grace of God, King of Prussia, and after the German princes and free cities have unanimously appealed to us to renew the Imperial dignity, which has been in abeyance for more than sixty years [since the end of the Holy Roman Empire] ... hereby inform
5 you that we regard it as our duty to the whole Fatherland to respond to this summons of the allied German princes and free cities and assume the German imperial title. May God grant to us and to our successors to the Imperial crown that we may be defenders of the German Empire at all times, not in military conquests, but in the works of peace,
10 in the sphere of national prosperity, freedom and civilisation.

William proclaimed Emperor

After these praiseworthy sentiments, the ceremony continued despite a little difficulty about the title. William had set his heart on '*Kaiser* (Emperor) of Germany', but as part of a deal made with the King of Bavaria to gain his support, Bismarck had agreed that the title should be 'German Kaiser'. The situation was saved by the Grand Duke of Baden, William's son-in-law, who neatly got round the problem by shouting out 'Long live his Imperial and Royal Majesty, Kaiser William'. William was not amused. Gravely displeased, he pointedly ignored Bismarck as the royal party left the platform.

Bismarck could afford to disregard William's displeasure, for he had achieved his aim. The fact that William had been proclaimed German Emperor at Versailles was a bitter pill for the French to swallow, and added to the humiliation of the surrender which came ten days later.

b) The Treaty of Frankfurt

The peace treaty between France and Germany was finally signed at Frankfurt in May 1871. German troops were to remain in eastern France until a heavy fine of £200 million had been paid, and Alsace and the eastern half of Lorraine were annexed to Germany. These harsh terms caused consternation in France. The Mayor of Strasburg, in Alsace, died of shock on hearing them. The peace terms were to lead to long-lasting enmity between France and Germany.

Why did Bismarck impose such a humiliating treaty on France, so different from the one which ended the Seven Weeks' War with Austria?

Alsace and Lorraine were rich in iron ore and good agricultural land, but Bismarck's interest in them was not essentially economic. Although a good case could be made for including Alsace in the German Reich, since Strasburg had been an Imperial City in the days of the old Holy Roman Empire, Lorraine was very French and it might have been better left unannexed. But there were good strategic reasons for taking both provinces. Bismarck believed that French defeat, irrespective of the peace terms, turned France into an irreconcilable enemy. He thus wished to ensure that she was so weakened that she could pose no threat to Germany in the future. The fortresses of Metz and Strasburg were crucial. Metz, in Moltke's view, was worth the equivalent of an army of 120,000 men. Moreover, during the war, the German press had portrayed France as the guilty party. Justly defeated, most Germans now believed she needed to be punished. One way of doing this was to annex territory, and 'geographical considerations' dictated that Alsace-Lorraine should be the territory chosen. The problem was that the new Reich would now have to cope with French desire for revenge. 'What we have gained by arms in half a year, we must protect by arms for half a century', said von Moltke.

c) Conclusion

The years 1870 and 1871 were dramatic for Bismarck and Europe, with France defeated, Germany united as an Empire and the balance of power in Europe totally altered. How much was this due to Bismarck?

It is possible to argue that Bismarck did not make Germany: rather Germany made Bismarck. A variety of factors – German nationalism, Prussian economic growth, the international situation in the 1860s, the Prussian army – were such that Bismarck was able to gain the credit for bringing about a unification which may well have developed naturally, whoever had been in power. However, whatever view is taken about the 'inevitability' of German unification, it is clear that it happened as it did and when it did largely as a result of Bismarck's actions. His precise aims baffled contemporaries and continue to baffle historians. It is difficult to disentangle his motives and to decide how far he planned ahead. While it is probably wrong to believe he came to power in 1862 with a master plan for German unification, it is equally wrong to imagine that he had no long-term objectives and fumbled his way through events simply by good luck. He manipulated situations even if he did not always create them. He had clear aims but the exact means of achieving them were left to short-term decisions based on the situation at the time. Perhaps his main skill as a diplomat lay in his ability to isolate his enemy. He was not essentially a warmonger. For Bismarck, wars were a risky means to an end. However, confident in the strength of the Prussian army, he was prepared in 1866 and in 1870 to engineer war to achieve his end. Having created a united Germany, the main question now was whether he would be able to deal with the domestic and foreign problems resulting from the unification process.

Working on Chapter 4

This chapter is concerned with the relationship between Bismarck and Napoleon III as much as between Prussia and France. Construct a diagram summarising the main events and points of this chapter.

Answering structured and essay questions on Chapter 4

The chances are that you will use evidence from this chapter and the previous one to answer specific questions about Bismarck and the unification of Germany. Three typical examples of such questions are:

How much did Bismarck's success from 1862 to 1870 depend on the errors and misjudgements of others?

How far was the unification of Germany achieved between 1862 and 1870 due to Bismarck's diplomacy?

Assess Bismarck's contribution to German unification.

All these questions are of the same basic type. They require you to construct a two part answer. One part argues, 'Yes ... in these ways/to this extent'. The other part argues, 'No ... in these ways/to this extent'. Look at the first question. In this case the approach would be, 'Yes, Bismarck's success was largely/to some extent due to the errors of others because ...', *but* other factors were also important, such as ...'. Make a list of the reasons to support the argument that Bismarck's success was due to the errors of others. Then make a second list, this time of the other factors involved in what you consider their order of importance, with supporting statements.

Source-based questions on Chapter 4

Source A: Telegraph message sent by a secretary of the King from Ems to Bismarck

1   Ems, July 13, 1870
    His Majesty writes to me: 'Count Benedetti [the French ambassador] spoke to me on the promenade to demand from me, finally in a very importunate manner, that I should authorize him to telegraph at once
5   that I bound myself for all future time never again to give my consent if the Hohenzellerns should renew their candidature. I refused at last somewhat sternly, as it is neither right nor proper to undertake engagements of this kind for all time. I told him that I had as yet received no news, and as he was earlier informed from Paris and Madrid than myself,
10 he could see clearly that my government had no more interest in the matter.' His Majesty has since received a letter from Prince Charles Anthony [Leopold's father]. His Majesty, having told Count Benedetti that he was awaiting news from the Prince, has decided not to receive Count Benedetti again, but only to let him be informed through an aide-
15 de-camp: 'That his Majesty has now received from the Prince confirmation of the news which Benedetti had already received from Paris, and had nothing further to say to the ambassador'. His Majesty leaves it to your Excellency to decide whether Benedetti's fresh demand and its rejection should be at once communicated to our ambassadors, to
20 foreign nations and to the press'.

Source B: Bismarck's *Memoirs*, written in the 1890s:

1   In view of the attitude of France, our national sense of honour compelled us, in my view, to go to war: and if we did not act according to the demands of this feeling, we should lose the entire impetus towards our national development won in 1866 ... Under this conviction I made
5   use of the royal authorisation to publish the contents of the telegram; and in the presence of my two guests reduced the telegram by striking out words, but without adding or altering, to the following form: 'After

the news of the renunciation of the Hereditary Prince of Hohenzollern
had been officially communicated to the Imperial government of France
10 by the Royal Government of Spain, the French ambassador further
demanded of His Majesty the King, at Ems, that he would authorize him
to telegraph to Paris that His Majesty the King bound himself for all
time never again to give his consent, should the Hohenzollerns renew
their candidacy. His Majesty the King, thereupon decided not to receive
15 the French ambassador again, and sent the aide-de-camp on duty to tell
him that His Majesty had nothing further to communicate to the ambassador.'

1. Study Source B
Explain Bismarck's comment: 'if we did not act according to the demands
of this feeling, we should lose the entire impetus towards our national
development won in 1866'. (3 marks)

2. Study Sources A and B.
With reference to your own knowledge, explain the importance of the
differences between the original Ems telegram and Bismarck's shorter version. (7 marks)

3. Study Sources A and B and use your own knowledge.
To what extent was the Franco-Prussian War the result of long-term planning on Bismarck's part? (15 marks)

5 Bismarck's Germany: 1871–90

POINTS TO CONSIDER

Bismarck dominated Germany for the two decades after 1870. His prestige as the creator of the new Reich was enormous and Emperor William I trusted him on most issues. What were Bismarck's aims after 1871 in both domestic and foreign policies? What problems did he face? How successful was he in dealing with these problems and achieving his aims?

KEY DATES

1871 January	German Empire proclaimed.
1872–3	May Laws.
1873	Three Emperors' League.
1875–8	Balkan Crisis.
1878 June–July	Congress of Berlin.
October	Anti-Socialist law passed.
1879	Dual Alliance.
1881	Three Emperors' Alliance.
1882	Triple Alliance.
1883	Sickness Insurance Act.
1884	Accident Insurance Act.
1887	Reinsurance Treaty with Russia.
1888	Death of William I.
1889	Old age pensions introduced.
1890	Kaiser Wilhelm II dismissed Bismarck.

1 The German Empire

KEY ISSUE Who controlled the Reich?

a) The German Constitution

The German Empire was proclaimed on 18 January 1871 in the palace of Versailles in France. King William I of Prussia became the new German emperor, or Kaiser, with Bismarck as his imperial chancellor. The constitution of the Reich essentially incorporated the main provisions of the constitution of the North German Confederation, drawn up by Bismarck in 1867. Germany was to be a federal state. Powers and functions were divided between the central, or federal, government and 25 state governments. While no longer

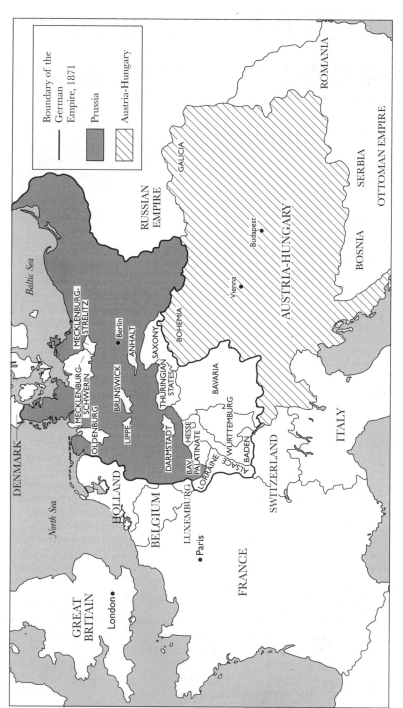

Map of the German Empire

EMPEROR
- Always the King of Prussia
- Could appoint and dismiss the Chancellor
- Could dissolve the Reichstag
- Controlled foreign policy
- Could make treaties and alliances
- Commanded the army
- Could declare war and make peace
- Supervised the execution of all Federal laws
- Possessed the right to interpret the constitution

CHANCELLOR
- Chief Minister of the Reich
- Not responsible to Reichstag, only to the Emperor
- He decided upon Reich policy outlines
- Chaired sessions of the Bundesrat
- Could 'hire and fire' State Secretaries responsible for the various government ministries
- Could ignore resolutions passed by the Reichstag
- Office was normally combined with the Minister-Presidency of Prussia

FEDERAL
Centralized government with specific responsibilities for the Reich as a whole, e.g. foreign affairs, defence, and criminal law, customs, coinage, railways, postal service

REICH GOVERNMENT

STATE
Regional government with special responsibilities for individual states, e.g. education, transport, direct taxation, police, local justice, health

BUNDESRAT
- The Federal Council
- Comprised 58 members nominated by State assemblies
- Its consent was required in the passing of new laws
- Theoretically able to change the constitution
- A vote of 14 against a proposal constituted a veto
- Prussia had 17 of the 58 seats, Bavaria 6, the smaller states one each
- In theory, it had extensive powers and practice. It actually rubber-stamped the Chancellor's policies

REICHSTAG
- The National Parliament
- Elected by all males over 25 years of age
- It could accept or reject legislation but power to initiate new laws was negligible
- State Secretaries were excluded from membership of Reichstag – not responsible to it
- Members were not paid
- Could approve or reject the budget
- Elected every 5 years (unless dissolved)

The German Constitution

sovereign or free to break away, the states preserved their own constitutions, rulers, parliaments and administrative systems. (See page 100) While the southern states retained some special internal rights, these were mainly decorative.

The German political system defies classification. Historians have variously described the Reich as a military monarchy, a sham-constitutional state, a semi-autocracy, or a constitutional monarchy. Arguably, it was all of these – and more! The complex, hybrid system can be seen (positively) as creating a delicate equilibrium with the key institutions keeping each other in check; it can also be seen (negatively) as creating major tensions, not least between monarchical and parliamentary claims to power, and between federal and state power.

As German emperor, the Prussian king was head of the imperial executive and civil service and supreme warlord of all the armed forces of the Empire. Prussia possessed 60 per cent of Germany's population and two-thirds of its territory. She returned 235 deputies out of a total of 397 in the Reichstag. She could block any unwelcome constitutional amendments in the Bundesrat. Not surprisingly, the Prussian aristocracy enjoyed a dominant position in the political, military and administrative structure of the Reich.

However, for all the complaints about a 'Prussianisation' of Germany, the identity of 'old Prussia' was significantly diluted by its integration into the Reich. Prussia could no longer be governed without consideration of the wider interests of Germany. Non-Prussians held important posts in government, both in the Reich as a whole and also in Prussia. It was the new German Reich, not Prussia, that now engaged the loyalties of most Germans. Many of Bismarck's former friends among the Prussian *Junker* class found it hard to forgive him for weakening Prussia.

b) Bismarck as Imperial Chancellor

After 1871 Bismarck was Prussian prime minister and foreign minister and Reich chancellor. As such, he exercised most of the powers ascribed to the crown in the constitution, including presiding over the Bundesrat. Bismarck's influence over William gave him an immensely strong position which he exploited. Loathing the existence of any rival authority, he ensured that other ministers were little more than senior clerks, carrying out his orders. There was no form of collective government and nothing which resembled an imperial cabinet. His reluctance to initiate subordinates into his thought processes, as well as his mistrust of potential rivals, encouraged him to rely more and more on his son Herbert, who was Secretary of State of the Foreign Office from 1886.

After 1871 Bismarck exerted a tight grip over all aspects of policy, foreign and domestic, in the Reich and in Prussia. So great was his influence that he is sometimes depicted as a dictator. However, there were practical and theoretical limitations to his power, especially in domestic affairs. The fact that Germany was a federal state reduced his influence. The Reichstag was another constraint. His long absences from Berlin (he liked to spend time on his country estates) and his poor health (often stomach troubles arising from over-eating and over-drinking) reduced his control of day-to-day decision-making. Many contemporaries viewed him with awe – a legend in his own lifetime. Recent historians have often been less impressed. They have represented him as more a lucky opportunist than a master-planner. They have also drawn attention to his less desirable attributes – his vindictiveness, his intolerance of criticism, and his frequent use of threats and bullying to get his way. It should be said that these methods did not always succeed. After 1871 he was persistently thwarted in his efforts to shape the domestic developments of the Reich.

c) How Democratic was Germany?

Bismarck was anxious for political power in Germany to remain in traditional hands – in those of the Emperor, his army officers, his ministers – and particularly with Bismarck himself. Arguably the constitution gave little opportunity for the exercise of democracy. Bismarck regarded the Reichstag with some disdain – as a collection of squabbling politicians who did not reflect popular opinion. However, the Reichstag could withhold consent to legislation and money bills. It was thus able to exert influence, if only of a negative kind. The urgent need for legislation to establish an economic and legal framework for the Empire ensured it played a significant role. Universal male suffrage promoted the development of mass political parties with popular appeal (see table on page 106). While these parties were in no position to form governments, Bismarck could not afford to ignore them. Although under no constitutional obligation to adopt policies approved by the Reichstag, he did need to secure support for his own legislative proposals. Bismarck grudgingly accepted that the co-operation of a popularly elected body was almost essential for the smooth-running of a modern state. Characteristically, however, he was only ready to work with the Reichstag on condition that it accepted his proposals or some compromise acceptable to him. If agreement could not be reached, he usually dissolved the Reichstag and called for fresh elections. He was prepared to use all the means at his disposal, not least the exploitation of international crises, to swing public opinion in elections to secure the passage of contentious legislation. He frequently made his opponents look like traitors.

Reichstag politicians have often been criticised by historians for failing to do more to exploit their potential power. However, they faced a difficult task. The balance of power was tilted sharply in favour of the monarchy and most Germans remained deeply respectful of authority, believing that it was right and proper that the Emperor, or his chancellor, should rule. There was no widespread conviction that power should be in the hands of the political party which happened to have a majority of seats in the Reichstag. Even members of the more extreme left-wing parties did not expect the Reichstag to exercise much control over government. The most that they hoped for was that it would have some influence on government decisions. Perhaps these hopes were realised. What is striking is how troublesome the Reichstag was for Bismarck, criticising and often thwarting his plans. Indeed, historians may have over-emphasised the way that the Reichstag bowed to Bismarck and not emphasised enough the way that he bowed to Reichstag pressure. On several occasions in the 1880s he explored the possibility of changing the constitution – proof of the Reichstag's influence. The Reichstag was thus neither a sovereign parliament nor simply a pliant instrument under Bismarck's control. It was something in between. It acquired a genuine popular legitimacy and became a focal point for those whom Bismarck saw as 'enemies of the state' – Poles, Catholics and Socialists.

d) The Role of the Army

The army played an important role in the Reich, as it had done in Prussia, and generals had a huge influence on government policy. Officers owed personal loyalty to the Emperor, not the state. The system of conscription ensured that all German men served for two to three years in the army. This gave the officers ample opportunity to build on the values already inculcated at school – discipline, pride in military institutions, and love of the fatherland. As the creator of the Reich, the army had a special place in the minds of most Germans. After 1871 it was still taken for granted that the army's needs must always come first and that the highest virtues were military ones. Uniforms brought exaggerated respect and obedience and both Bismarck and the Kaiser always wore uniform in public. The Kaiser at least had the excuse that he was Commander-in-Chief of the imperial forces as well as those of Prussia. Bismarck clearly believed that he gained respect through association with the victorious army. Given that the military budget was not subject to annual approval, the army was virtually independent of Reichstag control.

e) German Disunity

The new Reich was far from united. Each state had its own traditions. Each also had very real powers over education, justice and religious matters. Over 60 per cent of the population were Protestant but Catholicism was strong in Alsace-Lorraine, in south-west Germany, in the Rhineland and among the Poles. 10 per cent of the Reich's population were non-German minorities. There were also economic and social divisions – between rich and poor, and between the industrial-ising north and west and the predominantly rural south and east. Thus a major problem was to unite Germany in fact as well as in theory.

f) German Economic and Social Development

	1870		1890
Population	41m.	Germany	49m.
	32m.	Britain	38m.
	36m.	France	38m.
Coal (m. tons)	38	Germany	89
	118	Britain	184
	13	France	26
Steel (m. tons)	0.3	Germany	2.2
	0.6	Britain	3.6
	0.08	France	0.6
Iron ore (m. tones)	2.9	Germany	8
	14	Britain	14
	2.6	France	3.5

German production: 1870–90

The results of the war against France provided a direct stimulus to the German economy. Alsace-Lorraine, for example, contained Europe's largest deposits of iron ore and production increased rapidly after 1871. The injection of the French indemnity payments into the German economy (see page 94) helped cause a spectacular if short-lived boom, especially in the building and railway industries. The boom assisted German banks which, in turn, provided capital for new industries such as electricity and chemicals. After 1873 the boom ended and some industries suffered hardship. Even so, industrial growth rate averaged about 3 per cent a year between 1873 and 1890. Coal production soared, steel production increased by some 700 per cent and the railway network doubled.

Germany's educational system is often seen as the basis for her economic success. In terms of elementary education she led the world. Her rate of illiteracy in the 1870s was just over 1 per cent, com-pared with 33 per cent in Britain. Schools were used to inculcate not just literacy, but also nationalist sentiments and respect for authority.

Germany's population grew from 41 million in 1871 to 49 million by 1890. There was a baby boom and an increase in life expectancy. The population growth would have been higher but 2 million Germans emi-grated – mainly to the USA. Towns experienced the greatest growth. Many doubled – or trebled – in size, thanks largely to migration from rural areas. Some areas, like Bavaria, remained in a sort of agrarian time-warp while others, like the Ruhr, experienced rapid industrialisation.

German society, despite all the economic changes, seems to have remained divided along traditional class lines. What mobility there was tended to be within a class rather than between different classes. The higher levels of the civil service and the army remained predominantly the preserve of the nobility. The most direct threat to the nobility's supremacy came from wealthy industrialists who generally tried to emulate, rather than supersede, the nobles. While the middle classes were expanding, the mass of the population were agricultural or industrial workers. For many farm labourers life was hard and industrial employment seemed an attractive option. Thus there was a drift to the cities, even though the living and working conditions of the proletariat remained poor.

2 Bismarck's Domestic Policies

KEY ISSUE How successful was Bismarck in domestic terms?

a) The Liberal Era (1871–9)?

It is customary to divide Bismarck's domestic policies into two quite distinct phases: a 'liberal era' pre-1879; and a conservative era thereafter. This is simplistic. Recent research has shown that the 'turning point' in 1878–9 was not as sudden, drastic or as important as was once imagined. After 1871 Bismarck, who claimed to stand above party or sectional interest, needed a parliamentary majority. Although he was by no means a true liberal, he had little alternative but to work with the National Liberals – easily the strongest party in the Reichstag for most of the 1870s (see table on page 106). In some respects the middle-class National Liberals were ideal allies. Most of them applauded Bismarck's success in creating a united Germany and were eager to help him consolidate national unity. In the early 1870s, the so-called 'foundation time', a much useful legislation was passed, getting rid of a great deal of legal and economic anomalies. A national system of currency was introduced, a Reichsbank was created, all internal tariffs were abolished and there was much legal standardisation. The National Liberals and Bismarck also united against the Catholic Church (see below).

However, relations between Bismarck and the National Liberals were always uneasy. Politically Bismarck did not agree with their hopes for the extension of parliamentary government. He disliked having to rely on them to ensure the passage of legislation and became increasingly irritated as they opposed a number of his proposals. The army budget was a particular bone of contention. In 1867 Bismarck and the National Liberals agreed that the military budget should remain at a fixed level outside Reichstag control until 1872. During the Franco-Prussian War the fixed budget was extended until

Party	Number of seats in Reichstag (1871–90)							
	1871	*1874*	*1877*	*1878*	*1881*	*1884*	*1887*	*1890*
The National Liberals	125	155	128	99	47	51	99	42

The National Liberals: The main support for this part came from the Protestant middle class. The party had two principal aims: (a) the creation of a strong nation-state and (b) the encouragement of a liberal constitutional state; the former in practice being the priority. Until 1878 the National Liberals were Bismarck's most reliable Reichstag allies.

The Centre Party	58	91	93	94	100	99	98	106

The Centre Party: This party defended the interests of the Catholic Church.

The Social Democratic Party (SDP)	2	9	12	9	12	24	11	35

The Social Democratic Party (SDP): Having close links with the trade unions, this was predominantly a working-class party. It fought for social reforms.

The German Conservative Party	57	22	40	59	50	78	80	73

The German Conservative Party: This party was mainly composed of Prussian landowners. Sceptical about the unification of Germany, it came to support Bismarck after 1878.

The Free Conservatives	37	33	38	57	28	28	41	20

The Free Conservatives: Drawn from a wider geographical and social base than the German Conservatives, the party contained not just landowners but also industrialists and professional and commercial interests. It offered Bismarck steady support.

The Progressives	47	50	52	39	115	74	32	76

The Progressives: A liberal party but one which, unlike the National Liberals, remained opposed to Bismarck's pursuit of a powerful nation-state at the expense of liberal constitutional principles.

National Groups (i.e. Alsatians, Poles, Danes)	14	30	30	30	35	32	29	27

Guelphs	9	4	10	4	10	11	4	11

Guelphs: Hanoverians who were supporters of the deposed King George.

Germany's political parties

1874. In 1874 Bismarck presented a law which laid down that an army of over 400,000 men would be automatically financed by federal expenditure. Given that 80 per cent of all federal expenditure was spent on the army, this threatened to seriously reduce the Reichstag's monetary powers. The measure was thus opposed by the National Liberals. Bismarck accused them of trying to undermine German military strength and threatened to call new elections. The National Liberals shrank from a constitutional conflict similar to that which had brought Bismarck to power in 1862. A compromise was reached. The military budget was fixed for seven years at a time, rather than voted for annually or fixed permanently. This was a major diminution of the Reichstag's power.

b) The Kulturkampf

Much of the 1870s was dominated by Bismarck's clash with the Catholic Church – the *Kulturkampf* (the 'struggle for culture' or the 'struggle for civilisation'). There were a number of reasons for this clash. Two-thirds of Germans, mainly those in Prussia and the north, were Protestant. One-third – Poles, Rhinelanders and southern Germans – were Catholic. In the late nineteenth century Church and State came into conflict in several countries. In 1864 Pope Pius IX's *Syllabus of Errors* had condemned as erroneous every major principle for which liberals stood. In 1870 the Vatican Council enunciated the doctrine of papal infallibility. This ruled that papal pronouncements on matters of faith and morals could not be questioned. These measures aroused great alarm in liberal circles. It seemed that Pius had declared moral war. Many of the most enlightened men of the time believed that the future of mankind was at stake. It seemed certain that militant Catholicism would interfere in the domestic affairs of states and support reactionary causes.

German Catholics, aware that they were a minority in an essentially Protestant state, formed their own party, the Centre Party, in 1870. In 1871 this party won 58 seats and became the second largest party in the Reichstag. It was unique among German parties in drawing its support from all social strata. It favoured greater self-rule for the component states of the Reich. It also objected to state interference in the Church's traditional sphere of influence – education.

Bismarck, a sincere Protestant, had little affection for Catholicism and soon came to view the Catholic minority with suspicion. His greatest concern in domestic policy was to unify and consolidate the new Reich. He was suspicious of minorities, which might threaten the Protestant, Prussianised government he had created and he saw plots and subversive activities everywhere. Many of the national minorities – the French in the west and the Poles in the east – who had no wish to be within the Reich were Catholic. So were Germans in the southern states, many of whom still tended to identify with Austria rather than with Prussia. So too were the Rhinelanders, some of whom still resented being 'Prussian' (despite being part of Prussia since 1815).

Bismarck saw the success of the Centre Party in 1871 as a grave danger to the unity of the new Empire. He thought that the Party would encourage civil disobedience among Catholics whenever the policies of the state conflicted with those of the Church. His suspicions deepened when he observed how rapidly the party became a rallying point for opponents of the Empire. Bismarck tried repeatedly to persuade the Vatican and the German bishops to withdraw support from the Centre Party. Only in 1872, when it was clear that these attempts had failed, did he sever diplomatic relations with the Vatican and intensify the campaign against the Catholic Church, with the intention of subordinating Church to state. Whether he really believed that the anti-Prussian political alignment in the Reichstag was a Vatican-inspired conspiracy of malcontents bent on destroying the Reich is debatable. But the *Kulturkampf* was widely understood at the time to be a war against internal opponents of unification.

It may be that the *Kulturkampf* was little more than a calculated political ploy on Bismarck's part: to put himself at the head of a popular, Protestant crusade which would be widely supported by the National Liberals and by the conservative elites in Prussia. It certainly enabled him to work closely with the National Liberals in the 1870s. They believed the *Kulturkampf* was a battle for progress against the forces of reaction.

Some 5,000 Catholics – they were known as 'Old Catholics' – refused to accept the decree on papal infallibility and broke with the Church. When Old Catholic teachers and professors were dismissed by Catholic bishops, Bismarck had an excellent excuse to attack the Catholic Church. Maintaining that the Prussian government was committed to the principle of religious toleration, he condemned the actions of the Catholic Church in a series of newspaper articles in 1872. This marked the start of the *Kulturkampf.*

While the *Kulturkampf* was centred on Prussia and directed against the Catholics of the Rhineland and Poland, its effects were felt throughout the Reich and legislation against the Church was passed by both the Prussian Landtag and the Reichstag. In 1872 Catholic schools were brought directly under the supervision of the state. In 1872 the Reichstag forbade the Jesuit order, whose members had always been great teachers and supporters of Papal authority, to set up establishments in Germany and empowered state governments to expel individual Jesuits. In May 1873 Dr Falk, the Prussian Minister of Religion and Education, introduced a package of measures known as the May Laws. These aimed to bring the Catholic Church under state control. All candidates for the priesthood now had to attend a secular university before commencing training, and all religious appointments became subject to state approval. In 1874 obligatory civil marriage was introduced in Prussia. Clergy could be fined, imprisoned and expelled if they failed to comply with the May Laws. In 1875 the *Kulturkampf* reached a climax with laws empowering Prussia to suspend subsidies to the Church in dioceses or parishes where the clergy resisted the new legislation and all religious orders, except nursing orders, were dissolved. The legislation was enforced vigorously in Prussia by Falk. By 1876 all but two of the 12 Prussian Catholic bishops were in exile or under house arrest and more than a 1,000 priests were suspended from their posts.

The results of the *Kulturkampf* were not at all what Bismarck had hoped. Attempts to repress Catholicism met with considerable opposition in Catholic areas. Only 30 out of 10,000 Prussian Catholic priests submitted to the May Laws. Catholic communities sheltered defiant priests, fought to resist discriminatory measures and fiercely maintained their religious culture and identity. Indeed, it was soon clear that the Church throve on persecution. Bismarck's hope of destroying the Centre Party backfired: the *Kulturkampf* strengthened rather than weakened his political opponents. In 1871 the Centre Party won 58 seats: in 1874 it won 91 seats. Bismarck's plan to head a popular Protestant crusade also failed to materialise. Protestants opposed some of the *Kulturkampf* legislation because it limited the influence of the Protestant – as well as the Catholic – Church in education.

By 1878 Bismarck accepted that the *Kulturkampf* had failed. He had underestimated the enemy: the Catholic Church had greater strength and more popular support than he had bargained for. By opening up a rift between the Reich and its Catholic subjects, the *Kulturkampf* had increased disunity, not removed it. Anxious to have the Centre Party on his side against a potentially worse enemy, Socialism, he was ready to cut his losses and end the *Kulturkampf*. His opportunity came with the death of Pope Pius IX in 1878. Pius's successor Leo XIII was conciliatory and direct negotiations led to improved relations between Bismarck and the Church. Falk was symbolically dismissed in 1879 and some of the anti-Catholic measures were repealed: exiled clergy, for example, were allowed to return. However, the Catholic Church did not win a complete victory. Many of the May Laws remained in force: for example, civil marriage remained compulsory, Jesuits were forbidden to enter Germany, and the State continued to oversee all permanent Church appointments. Having suffered a defeat, Bismarck withdrew from a dangerous battlefield. Typically, he sought to turn failure to advantage, by henceforward harnessing Catholic political power in the Reichstag to the support of conservative, protectionist and anti-Socialist measures.

c) Economic Protectionism

In the early 1870s Bismarck left economic matters in the hands of Delbruck, a capable administrator who continued the free trade policies of the *Zollverein*. Support for free trade was an essential principle of most National Liberals. In 1879, however, Bismarck ditched both free trade and the National Liberals. Aligning himself with the Conservative and Centre parties, he supported the introduction of tariffs, or customs duties, to protect German industry and farming. Historians continue to debate his motives. Some think he acted simply out of political opportunism. Others, more convincingly, argue that he believed protectionism to be in the best economic interests of the Reich. As early as 1877 he had had tried to persuade National Liberals to abandon their opposition to tariff protection.

There were strong economic and financial reasons for introducing tariffs. In the late 1870s German agriculture suffered from the effects of a series of bad harvests and from the importation of cheap wheat from the USA and Russia. As the price of wheat fell, German farmers suffered. As a landowner himself, Bismarck understood the dangers of a prolonged agrarian depression. He also feared that if Germany was reliant on foreign grain, she would be seriously weakened in time of war. Protectionism would aid German self-sufficiency. Moreover, after 1873 industry experienced a difficult period. The slow-down in growth helped to produce a crisis of confidence in economic liberalism. Industrialists and workers looked to the government to protect their interests and alleviate their distress. The adoption of protective tariffs by France, Russia and Austria-Hungary in the late 1870s seemed to make it all the more desirable to follow suit. Finally, the federal government's revenue, raised from customs duties and indirect taxation, was proving woefully inadequate to cover the growing costs of armaments and administration. In order to make up the deficit, supplementary payments were made by individual states, a situation Bismarck found distasteful. He hoped that new tariffs would give the federal government a valuable extra source of income ensuring that it was financially independent of both the states and the Reichstag.

Bismarck also realised there were political advantages in abandoning free trade. By the late 1870s German landowners and industrialists were clamouring for protective tariffs. By espousing protectionist policies, Bismarck could win influential support. He had never been particularly friendly with the National Liberals, whose insistence on parliamentary rights and refusal to pass anti-Socialist legislation had really begun to irritate him. Moreover, in the 1878 elections, the National Liberals lost some 30 seats. The combined strength of the two Conservative parties was now sufficient to outvote them in the Reichstag. In pursuing the protectionist case, popular with the Conservatives, Bismarck saw his chance to break with the National Liberals and broaden his political support.

By 1879 an all-party association for tariff reform, made up mostly of Conservatives and Centre Party members, had a majority in the

Reichstag. Bismarck now introduced a general tariff bill. He addressed the Reichstag in May 1879 as follows:

1 The only country [which persists in a policy of free trade] is England, and that will not last long. France and America have departed completely from this line; Austria instead of lowering her tariffs has made them higher; Russia has done the same ... Therefore to be alone the
5 dupe of an honourable conviction cannot be expected from Germany for ever. By opening wide the doors of our state to the imports of foreign countries, we have become the dumping ground for the production of those countries ... Since we have become swamped by the surplus production of foreign nations, our prices have been depressed;
10 and the development of our industries and our entire economic position has suffered in consequence. Let us finally close our doors and erect some barriers ... in order to reserve for German industries at least the home market, which because of German good nature, has been exploited by foreigners. The problem of a large export trade is
15 always a very delicate one; there are no new lands to discover, the world has been circumnavigated, and we can no longer find abroad new purchasers of importance to whom we can send our goods ... I see that those countries which have adopted protection are prospering, and that those countries which have free trade are deteriorating.

In July 1879 a tariff bill passed through the Reichstag and duties were imposed on imports. The political results were far-reaching. Bismarck had now firmly committed himself to the conservative camp. The National Liberal party splintered. Those who still believed in free trade and parliamentary government broke away, eventually uniting with the Progressives to form a new radical party in 1884. Other National Liberals remained loyal to Bismarck but he was no longer dependent on their backing. In that sense the 'Liberal era' was effectively at an end.

Historians continue to debate the economic effects of the abandonment of free trade. Arguably, protective tariffs consolidated the work of unification, by drawing north and south closer together, and accelerated the growth of a large internal market. Protection might have meant higher bread prices but this did not mean that German workers had lower living standards. Tariffs did serve to protect German jobs.

d) Bismarck and Socialism

The Universal German Workingmen's Association had been formed in Prussia in 1863 as a moderate organisation to help workers obtain more political power by peaceful means. In 1869 Bebel and Liebknecht founded the Social Democratic Workers' Party – a Marxist party committed to the overthrow of the bourgeoisie. In 1875 moderate and revolutionary socialists united to form the German Social

Democratic Party (or SDP). The party's declared aim was the overthrow of the existing order. But it also declared that it would use only
legal means in the struggle for economic and political freedom. The
new party called for nationalisation of banks, coal mines and industry
and for social equality. It won support from the growing number of
industrial workers.

Bismarck was hostile to socialists, regarding them as anarchic, revolutionary and little better than criminals. As with Catholicism, he
feared the international appeal of socialist ideology. How could one
be loyal both to an international organisation and to one's own
country? Rather than underestimating the enemy, as with the
Kulturkampf, it may be that he overestimated the socialist threat.
Socialists were not as strong nor as revolutionary as he feared and they
liked to appear. However, his fears were rational. Socialism was a
threat to the kind of society Bismarck intended to maintain. Socialists
did preach class warfare. Moreover, socialist support was growing.
The SPD won two seats in the Reichstag in 1871; in 1877 it had 12
seats and won nearly 500,000 votes.

In 1876 Bismarck tried to pass a bill preventing the publication of
socialist propaganda. It was defeated. Other measures to prosecute
the SDP also failed to get through the Reichstag. In 1878 an anarchist
tried to kill William I. The would-be assassin had no proven association with the SDP but Bismarck, like many of his contemporaries,
drew no clear distinction between anarchism and socialism and saw
the murder attempt as part of a 'red' conspiracy. But his efforts to
push through a bill against socialism were defeated by National
Liberal and Centre Party members, concerned about civil liberties. A
week later there was a second attempt on William's life, resulting in
the emperor being seriously wounded. Again the would-be assassin
had no direct SDP link. Bismarck criticised the National Liberals for
failing to pass the anti-socialist bill which might have protected the
emperor and, scenting political advantage, dissolved the Reichstag.
His manoeuvre succeeded. The electorate, shocked by the murder
attempts, blamed the SDP and the National Liberals. The SDP vote
fell from 493,000 in 1877 to 312,000, while the National Liberals lost
130,000 votes and 29 seats. Only by supporting anti-socialist legislation during the election campaign did they save themselves from a
heavier defeat. The Conservative parties gained 38 seats.

Bismarck now got his way in the new Reichstag. An anti-socialist
bill, supported by Conservatives and most National Liberals, was
passed in October 1878. Socialist organisations, including trade
unions, were banned, their meetings were broken up and their pub-
lications outlawed. Between 1878 and 1890 some 1,500 socialists were
imprisoned and a great many emigrated. However, the anti-Socialist
Law, far from eliminating socialism, served to rally the faithful and
fortify them in their beliefs. The SDP simply went underground.
Moreover, the Law did not prevent SDP members from standing for

election and speaking freely in both the Reichstag and state legislatures. After the dip in 1878, the SDP won increasing support. By 1890 it had over a million voters and 35 seats. Well-organised, it became a model for other European socialist parties. In short, Bismarck's attack on socialism was no more successful than his attack on the Church. His repressive measures may have helped increase support for the SDP and ensured that moderate and revolutionary socialist factions remained united.

e) State Socialism

Bismarck did not only use repression in his efforts to destroy socialism. He hoped to wean the working classes from socialism by introducing various welfare (state socialism) measures, designed to assist German workers at times of need. These measures may not have been as cynical as some of Bismarck's critics have implied. A devout Christian, Bismarck was conscious of a moral obligation to aid those in need. There was a strong paternalist tradition in Prussia and other parts of Germany, and a general belief, right and left, that one of the state's most important moral objectives was the promotion of the material well-being of its citizens. Bismarck, however, also hoped to win the support of the workers, thus cutting the ground from beneath the feet of the socialists. In a speech to the Reichstag in 1881 he said:

1 A beginning must be made with the task of reconciling the labouring classes with the state. A remedy cannot be sought only through the repression of socialist excesses. It is necessary to have a definite advancement in the welfare of the working classes. The matter of the
5 first importance is the care of those workers who are incapable of earning a living. Previous provision for guarding workers against the risk of falling into helplessness through incapacity caused by accident or age have not proved adequate, and the inadequacy of such provisions has been a main contributing cause driving the working classes to seek help
10 by joining the Social Democratic movement. Whoever has a pension assured to him for his old age is more contented and easier to manage than a man who has none.

ACTIVITY

1. What argument does Bismarck use to justify his decision to support state socialism?
2. What does Bismarck's line of argument suggest about the values and attitudes of the majority in the Reichstag?

In 1883 the first of his proposals for state socialism became law. The Sickness Insurance Act provided medical treatment and up to 13 weeks' sick pay to three million low-paid workers and their families. The workers paid two-thirds of the contribution and the employers one third. A worker who was permanently disabled or sick for more than 13 weeks was given protection by the Accident Insurance Act of 1884. This was financed wholly by the employers. In 1886 it was extended to cover seven million agricultural workers. Finally in 1889 came the Old Age and Disability Act which gave pensions to those over 70, and disablement pensions for those who were younger. This was paid for by workers, employers and the state.

Many historians regard state socialism as Bismarck's most important legacy. His scheme was the first of its kind in the world and became a model of social provision for other countries. However, his hopes that the working class could be won over were not fully realised. Whilst well received by some workers, others thought state socialism was a 'sham' particularly as the government still opposed the formation of trade unions. Many workers continued to labour under harsh conditions and, while such conditions persisted, the SDP was assured of a future. Bismarck, believing that employers must control their factories, opposed demands for state intervention to regulate working hours, limit child and female employment, and improve working conditions. Nevertheless, state socialism probably did make German workers 'more contented and easier to manage'.

f) Treatment of the National Minorities

Bismarck regarded the national minorities – the Danes, French and Poles – as potential 'enemies of the state'. He thus sought to reduce their political and social influence. The Polish language was outlawed in education and law courts. Alsace-Lorraine was not granted full autonomy after 1871. Instead it became a special region under direct imperial rule with a governor and Prussian civil servants. The German language was imposed in schools and local administration. However, Bismarck did not rely solely on repression. Those French people who were unhappy with German rule were allowed to leave. 400,00 had done so by 1914. The German governors of Alsace-Lorraine made great efforts to conciliate the French-speaking provinces. The national minorities problem was not solved. However, it does seem that the national minorities' alienation from the Reich probably lessened over the years. School, conscription and everyday experience 'Germanised' many minorities.

3 Bismarck's Foreign Policy: 1871–90

> **KEY ISSUE** How successful was Bismarck's foreign policy?

a) Bismarck's Aims

In Bismarck's view, Germany was a 'satiated power' after 1871 without further territorial ambitions. In consequence, he was not interested in attaching Austrian Germans to the new Reich. He believed that any attempt to disrupt the existing order of things by extending Germany's frontiers in any direction would unite the other great powers against her. Convinced that further wars could only threaten the security of the Reich, his main aim was to maintain peace. France seemed the main threat to peace. She would have resented her defeat in 1870–1 under any circumstances. The loss of Alsace-Lorraine merely sharpened the edge of that resentment. Many Frenchmen wanted revenge. France without allies did not pose a serious danger to Germany since Bismarck was confident that the German army could defeat her again if necessary. His main fear was that France might ally with either Russia or Austria. Germany might then have to fight a war on two fronts. He was determined to avoid this possibility by isolating France and remaining on good terms with both Russia and Austria. The main problem was that there was always the possibility of friction between Austria and Russia over the Balkans, where their interests were at variance.

The Balkans, the most troublesome area of Europe, presented major problems for Bismarck. The Turkish government's authority in many Balkan areas was only nominal. Peoples of various races and religions co-existed in a state of mutual animosity. The Slav peoples were becoming fiercely nationalistic. Russia sought to assist the Slavs to obtain independence from Turkey. She also sought to profit from Turkey's weakness by winning control of the Straits (the Bosphorous and Dardanelles). Austria was opposed to the expansion of Russian power so close to her territories. In addition, Russia's encouragement of Slav nationalism could serve as a dangerous example to national groups within the Habsburg Empire. Austria thus sought to maintain the Ottoman Empire. She feared that if the multi-national Ottoman Empire collapsed, her own similarly multi-national Empire might follow. Bismarck had no territorial ambitions in the Balkans: he once remarked that the area was not worth 'the healthy bones of a single Pomeranian musketeer'. However, if Austria and Russia fell out over the Balkans, Germany might have to choose between them. The fear was that the rejected suitor would find a willing ally in France.

Although Bismarck faced problems, he also had a strong hand. He enjoyed far more control in the handling of foreign affairs than in domestic matters. Germany was the greatest military power in Europe and her friendship was eagerly sought by Austria and Russia, in part because of their growing antagonism in the Balkans.

b) The Three Emperors' League and the 1875 War Scare

Austria-Hungary, fearing a German–Russian agreement, took the initiative in pressing for a Three Emperors' alliance. Following a meeting in 1872, the Emperors of Germany, Russia and Austria reached an agreement known as the Three Emperors' League or *Dreikaiserbund*. Given that the three powers found it hard to reach agreement on any concrete objectives, the terms were somewhat vague. The emperors identified republicanism and socialism as common enemies and promised to consult on matters of common interest or if a third power disturbed Europe's peace. While this was far from a cunning plan on Bismarck's part, it very much suited his purpose.

In the early 1870s France made determined efforts to throw off the effects of defeat. Her rapid military reorganisation and the prompt repayment of the war indemnity, ensuring the riddance of the German army of occupation by 1873, surprised and alarmed Bismarck. In 1875 he reacted to French recovery and rearmament by provoking a diplomatic crisis. He prohibited the export of horses to France and in April the *Berlin Post* carried an article 'Is War in Sight?' Bismarck expected that the other powers would similarly put pressure on France, discouraging her from further military expansion. He miscalculated. Britain and Russia warned Germany about her provocative actions, forcing Bismarck to offer assurances that Germany was not contemplating a war against France. The crisis thus ended in a diplomatic victory for France. Britain and Russia made it clear they would not allow Germany to destroy France.

c) The Balkan Crisis 1875–8

In 1875 Christian peasants in Bosnia and Herzegovina revolted against Turkish rule. In April 1876 the revolt spread to Bulgaria and in July Montenegro and Serbia declared war on Turkey. Thousands of Russian volunteers joined the Serbian army amidst a wave of popular pro-Slavonic fervour. There was thus pressure for Russian intervention in the Balkans. It was likely that Austria would oppose anything which smacked of Russian expansionism. Bismarck was thus concerned: he might have to choose between his *Dreikaiserbund* partners so presenting France with a potential ally. Determined to avoid taking sides, he had somehow to convince both Austria and Russia of Germany's goodwill, prevent them from quarrelling, and encourage them to find a solution to the problem.

Bismarck was helped by the fact that Tsar Alexander II and his Foreign Minister Gorchakov preferred international discussion to unilateral action. Austro-Hungarian Foreign Minister Andrassy tried to collaborate with Gorchakov in an attempt to end – or at least limit the effects of – the crisis. However, Turkish atrocities in 1876 in Bulgaria (some 10,000 Bulgarians were allegedly killed) changed the situation. The atrocities stirred public opinion in both Britain and Russia with important effects. In Britain Disraeli's government was temporarily prevented from pursuing the traditional British policy of supporting Turkey against Russia. In Russia the sufferings of the Bulgarians and the defeat of Serbian and Montenegrin forces enflamed Pan-Slavist sentiment to such an extent that the Tsarist government found itself under mounting pressure to intervene on the side of the Balkan rebels. In November 1876 Tsar Alexander II declared that if his 'just demands' for the protection of Balkan Christians were not agreed to by Turkey, and the other great powers would not support him, then he was prepared to act independently. Russian and Austrian policy was suddenly out of step and both turned to Germany for support. In December 1876 the Tsar asked for an assurance of German neutrality in the event of an Austro-Russian war. Bismarck was evasive. He similarly refused Andrassy's offer of an Austro-German alliance against Russia.

In January 1877 Russia managed to buy Austrian neutrality in the event of a Russo-Turkish war by agreeing that Austria would receive Bosnia-Herzegovina, and promising that no large state would be set up in the Balkans. In April Russia declared war on Turkey. Courageous Turkish defence of the fortress of Plevna deprived Russia of a quick victory. It also caused British opinion to swing back in favour of the heroic Turks. Plevna finally fell in December 1877 and the Russians were able to resume their advance. By January 1878 they threatened Constantinople. In March they imposed the severe San Stefano Treaty on the Turks. This treaty significantly improved Russia's position in the Balkans. European Turkey was to be reduced to small unconnected territories by the creation of a Big Bulgaria. Serbia, Montenegro and Romania were to be fully independent of Turkey. There was no mention of Austria taking Bosnia-Herzegovina.

The San Stefano Treaty confirmed Andrassy's worst fears that he been duped. The proposal to create a Big Bulgaria was seen as a cynical Russian attempt to establish a Balkan client state with a strategically important Aegean coastline. Austria mobilised her army. Britain summoned troops from India and despatched the fleet to Turkish waters. Faced with Austro-British hostility and the threat of a major war, which she was in no economic or military state to fight, Russia agreed to an international conference to revise the peace terms. Bismarck, somewhat reluctantly, offered his services as the 'honest broker'. He realised he was likely to be blamed by one or the other, or even by both, of his allies for their disappointments.

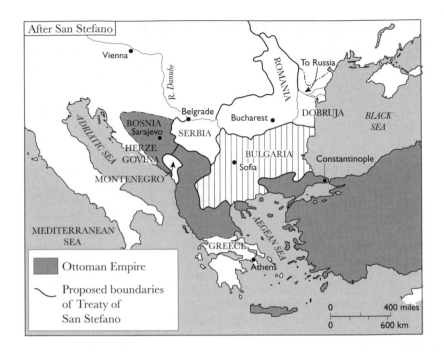

The Balkans: 1878

d) The Congress of Berlin: June–July 1878

The fact that the Congress – the most important meeting of the powers since 1856 – took place in Berlin was a sign of Germany's new power and Bismarck's prestige. Much preparatory work had been done before the Congress met: Russia had agreed to reduce the size of Bulgaria; Britain had agreed to guarantee Turkey's security in exchange for the island of Cyprus; the Sultan had promised to introduce reforms; and Britain had agreed to support Austria's claims to occupy Bosnia-Herzegovina. Despite these preliminary accords, the Congress was not all plain sailing. At critical moments, only Bismarck's energetic intervention saved the day.

By the Treaty of Berlin, Big Bulgaria was divided into three. The northern part, Bulgaria proper, was granted complete independence under Russian supervision. To the south the province of Eastern Roumelia was to have a form of self-government under Turkish suzerainty. The third part – Macedonia – was returned to Turkish rule. Russia recovered southern Bessarabia, from Romania, and gained Batun, a valuable port on the eastern edge of the Black Sea, from Turkey. Austria was to occupy Bosnia-Herzegovina while Britain gained Cyprus.

Perhaps Britain had best reason to be pleased with the Treaty of Berlin. Disraeli's firm stand had checked Russia and Cyprus was a useful acquisition. Russia, by contrast, felt she had suffered a humiliating diplomatic defeat. She had done all the fighting and then seen Britain and Austria-Hungary get away with some major spoils.

For Bismarck the Congress was a mixed blessing. His main desire – that of keeping peace – had been achieved. However, Russia blamed him for her diplomatic defeat. Alexander II described the Congress as 'a coalition of the European powers against Russia under the leadership of Prince Bismarck'. Russo-German relations quickly deteriorated. The introduction of German protective tariffs in 1879 did not help matters, given Russia's dependence on wheat exports to Germany. By 1878–9 the *Dreikaiserbund* was well and truly dead. Bismarck was now in a potentially dangerous position. There was suddenly the real possibility of a Franco-Russian alliance.

e) The Dual Alliance

In 1878–9 it seemed to Bismarck that Germany was faced with the stark choice of continuing Russian hostility or allying with her. An alliance would sacrifice his relationship with Austria and risk enmity with Britain. His response to the pressure from Russia was to put out feelers for an alliance with Austria. In October 1879 Bismarck and Andrassy agreed to the Dual Alliance. This committed both countries to resist Russian aggression. If Germany or Austria was at war with a third power, the other partner would remain neutral unless Russia intervened. The secret alliance was to last five years. However, the option to renew the arrangement was taken up so that it became the cornerstone of German foreign policy, lasting until 1918. The Dual Alliance was thus something of a 'landmark'. Previous treaties had usually been concluded on the eve of wars. This was a peacetime engagement. It encouraged other powers to negotiate similar treaties until all Europe was divided into pact and counter-pact.

Why did Bismarck agree to the Dual Alliance? In his *Reminiscences* he described it as the fruition of a grand design cherished since 1866. There is, in fact, no evidence that he had it in mind before 1879. In reality he acted on the spur of the moment to deal with an emergency. In 1879 the Dual Alliance provided Germany with an ally with whom she could weather the storm of Russian hostility. Bismarck chose to ally with Austria-Hungary rather than Russia partly because he felt she would be easier to control and partly because an alliance with a fellow German power was likely to be more popular in Germany, particularly with the Catholics, than an alliance with Russia. In truth, however, the Dual Alliance was only a temporary expedient to preserve the precarious balance of power in the Balkans and to compel a more friendly Russian attitude towards both Austria-Hungary and Germany. It was not a final choice between them. Bismarck never wavered in his belief that the *'entente á trois'* was Germany's best hope.

f) The Three Emperors' Alliance

Russia, alarmed at her isolation and not anxious to ally with republican France, soon turned back to Germany. However, more than 18 months elapsed before a new *Dreikaiserbund* was signed. This was partly due to problems arising from the death of Alexander II and the accession of Tsar Alexander III. Austria-Hungary was also opposed to the entire project. However, Andrassy finally yielded to Bismarck's pressure and in 1881 the Three Emperors' Alliance, a secret treaty of three years' duration, was signed. If Russia, Germany or Austria were at war with another power, the others would remain neutral. The three powers also agreed to keep the entrance to the Black Sea closed to foreign warships. Thus Britain would not be free to use the Straits whenever she wished. Nor would the three permit territorial changes in the Balkans without prior, mutual agreement. Instead, the Balkans were to be divided into 'spheres of influence'. Russian interests were recognised in the eastern portion, Austrian interests in the western.

Bismarck was delighted with the agreement. His confident assertion to Emperor William that Russia would return to the fold had come to pass and the conservative alliance was restored.

g) The Triple Alliance

Bismarck, hoping to divert French attention away from Alsace-Lorraine, encouraged France to embark on colonial expansion in

Africa and Asia. This had the added advantage of alienating France from Britain. In 1881 France seized Tunis. This angered Italy who had designs on the same territory. In 1881 Italy made overtures to Austria aimed at securing an alliance. Austria had little interest in the Italian bid for closer ties, but Bismarck, although having a poor opinion of Italy's strength, saw its potential. Bringing Italy closer to the Dual Alliance would deprive France of a potential ally. Accordingly, in 1882 the Triple Alliance was signed. If any of the signatories were attacked by two or more powers, the others promised to lend assistance. In the event of a war between Austria and Russia, Italy would remain neutral. If France attacked Germany, Italy would provide support to her partner. If Italy were attacked by France, both Germany and Austria agreed to back her. Italian leaders were pleased with the alliance. It conferred some prestige and there was the prospect that it would help her colonial ambitions. However, Bismarck carefully restrained Italy in Africa as he restrained Austria in the Balkans.

More alliances were in the offing. An Austrian agreement with Serbia in 1881 turned the country virtually into an Austrian satellite. An agreement with Romania followed in 1883. Austria-Hungary and Germany undertook to defend Romania, while Romania agreed to fight if Russia attacked Austria. The Three Emperors' Alliance was renewed in 1884. In 1884 Bismarck even managed to be on tolerably good terms with France. This was the zenith of Bismarck's 'system'.

h) Bismarck and Colonies

In 1881 Bismarck declared that 'so long as I am Chancellor we shall pursue no colonial policy'. However, in 1884–5 Germany acquired a large overseas Empire. Why did Bismarck change his mind?

In the early 1880s colonialism became fashionable. Many European nations were interested in carving up Africa. Enthusiastic pressure groups sprang up agitating for colonies on economic grounds and as a sign of national greatness. The German Colonial Union, founded in 1882 with support from major industrialists, did much to interest German public opinion in overseas expansion. Within Germany there was concern about the consequences of protectionist policies. Trading companies were complaining of being squeezed out of parts of Africa by foreign rivals. Bismarck hoped that colonies might benefit the German economy by providing new markets and raw materials. The absence of serious difficulties with either Russia or France enabled Bismarck to embark on an energetic colonial policy. Moreover, by putting pressure on Britain in the colonial field, Bismarck hoped to force her into adopting a more pro-German policy in European affairs.

Bismarck had also good political reasons to support German colonialism. The 1884 elections were in the offing. He needed an issue that would weaken the liberal parties. Colonialism was a convenient

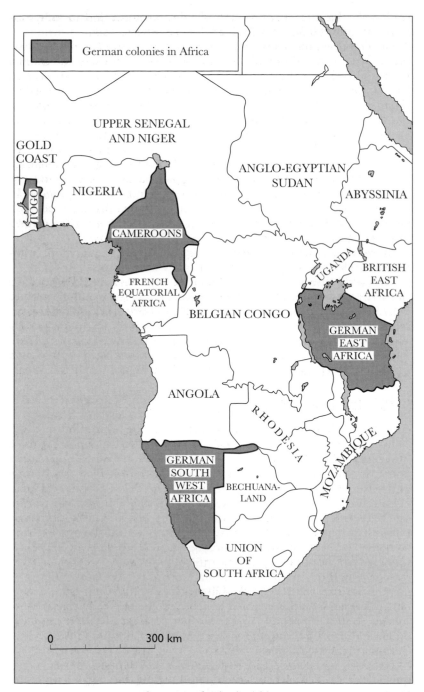

German colonies in Africa

stick with which to beat the Radicals and Socialists and to rally support. His ploy worked: the Radicals lost 38 seats in 1884.

In 1884 Bismarck deliberately picked quarrels with Britain over colonial claims in South-west Africa and sided with France in opposition to British plans in Egypt. Facing a Russian threat in central Asia, Britain had no wish to antagonise Germany and was not opposed to Germany acquiring colonies. Thus in 1884–5 Germany acquired South-West Africa, Togoland, the Cameroons, German East Africa and some Pacific islands – one million square miles of land in total.

Bismarck had a sharp eye for any new opportunity. In the mid-1880s he seriously considered the possibility of a lasting reconciliation with France as the best way of avoiding war on two fronts. Active co-operation with France in the colonial field was the first step. By picking quarrels with Britain over German colonial claims, he aligned Germany on France's side. However, better relations with France were short-lived. In 1886 General Boulanger became French War Minister and talked of a war to recover Alsace-Lorraine. Franco-German relations quickly deteriorated.

Bismarck's interest in colonial matters was short-lived. By 1887 he was resisting demands for further colonial expansion on the grounds of Germany's continental security. As relations with France and Russia deteriorated, he had no wish to alienate Britain. Thus he made substantial concessions to Britain when east Africa was partitioned in 1889. A German official observed that a 'good understanding with England means much more to Bismarck than the whole of east Africa'.

i) The Bulgarian Crisis

A crisis in Bulgaria in 1885–6 shattered the Three Emperors' Alliance, due for renewal in 1887. Austria and Russia again squared up against each other in the Balkans. Bismarck refused to take sides in the dispute. As Austro-Russian relations worsened, Bismarck's fears of France revived. Nationalistic feelings in France were whipped up by Boulanger. To make matters worse, pro-French ministers in Russia seemed to be exerting great influence over the Tsar. For domestic reasons, Bismarck may well have exaggerated the danger of war. However, he was clearly alarmed by the fear of a Franco-Russian alliance and felt that diplomatic precautions were needed to safeguard Germany.

In February 1887 the Triple Alliance was renewed on terms more favourable to Italy than those she obtained in 1882. Bismarck persuaded Austria to promise to consult Italy on all matters affecting the Balkans, the Adriatic and the Aegean. In March 1887, with Bismarck's full backing, Britain, Austria and Italy signed the First Mediterranean Agreement, committing themselves to the maintenance of the status quo in the eastern Mediterranean – an action that was clearly anti-Russian.

j) The Reinsurance Treaty

Events now turned in Bismarck's favour. France, suddenly cautious, avoided Russian feelers and conservative diplomats again won the upper hand in St Petersburg. Tsar Alexander III accepted their argument that an agreement with Germany was better than nothing and in June 1887 the Reinsurance Treaty was signed. By this, if either Russia or Germany were at war with a third power, the other would remain benevolently neutral. The provision would not apply to a war against Austria or France resulting from an attack on one of these two powers by either Russia or Germany. The Treaty, which did not contravene the Dual Alliance, can be seen as a masterpiece of diplomatic juggling on Bismarck's part. However, its importance should probably not be exaggerated. If not exactly a desperate stop-gap measure, it was hardly the cornerstone of Bismarck's system: indeed he seems to have attached little importance to it. It was simply another temporary expedient to remove his fears of a Franco-Russian alliance.

Russo-German relations did not improve much after 1887. Bismarck was partly to blame for this. In November 1887 he denied Russia access to the Berlin money market for loans to finance her industrialisation in order 'to remove the possibility that the Russians wage war against us at our cost'. In consequence, Russia simply turned to Paris where French financiers were eager to accommodate them. Nor did the Reinsurance Treaty necessarily reduce the danger of a clash over the Balkans. Indeed the Bulgarian situation continued to cause tension. Bismarck used all his influence to encourage Britain, Italy and Austria to sign the Second Mediterranean Agreement (December 1887), again guaranteeing the status quo in the Near East. In February 1888 he published the Dual Alliance, partly to warn Russia that Germany would stand by Austria if it came to war and partly to restrain Austria by making it clear that Germany's obligations were limited to a defensive war. The publication coupled with rumours of the Mediterranean Agreement persuaded Russia to hold her hand and the Bulgarian crisis finally fizzled out.

4 Bismarck's Fall

KEY ISSUE Why did Bismarck fall from power?

a) Threats to Bismarck's Position

The late 1880s were a difficult period for Bismarck. William I was in his eighties and his advancing years cast a shadow over Bismarck's plans. If William died, Crown Prince Frederick, a man of liberal views who was married to the eldest daughter of Queen Victoria, would ascend the throne. It seemed likely that he would dismiss Bismarck and appoint a liberal chancellor. This would be welcome to the Reichstag where a majority was no longer in Bismarck's pocket.

The friction between Bismarck and the Reichstag came to a head in 1887 over the renewal of the army grant or Septennates. The current Septennates were not due to expire until 1888 but the international situation alarmed the generals, who pressed for an early renewal. Thus in late 1886 Bismarck asked the Reichstag to agree to substantial military increases. The Reichstag agreed but only on condition that in future it was allowed to review military expenditure every three years, not every seven. Bismarck was furious. 'The German army is an institution which cannot be dependent on short-lived Reichstag majorities', he declared. Dissolving the Reichstag, he conjured up a picture of a revenge-seeking France, ready for war at any moment. Germany would remain in danger until the Septennates were passed and only the Conservatives and National Liberals could be relied upon to pass them. Bismarck's electoral stratagem worked. The Conservatives and National Liberals won an absolute majority in 1887 and the Septennates were passed.

b) William II and Bismarck

While William I lived Bismarck's hold on power was never in question. Their meetings were often stormy, emotional and noisy. They shouted, threw things, burst into tears and quarrelled for much of the time. But they understood each other. 'It is not easy to be the Emperor under such a Chancellor', William remarked, but he managed it successfully, mainly by letting Bismarck have his own way.

When William died in March 1888 he was succeeded briefly by his son Frederick. Frederick, however, died from cancer only three months later. Frederick's 29-year-old son William II then became Emperor. He was a convinced German nationalist and was totally committed to the belief that he ruled by Divine Right. 'Remember the German people are chosen by God. On me as the German Emperor, the spirit of God has descended. I am his weapon, his sword, his vice regent.' William's character was complex and full of contradictions. On the positive side, he was intelligent, talented, cultured and energetic. On the negative, he was overbearing, arrogant and erratic.

After Frederick's death, Bismarck's position seemed secure again. He had cultivated the prince's friendship for several years and in public William expressed his admiration for Bismarck. But a great gulf separated the two, not least age. Treating William in a condescending manner, Bismarck assumed he would not involve himself much in matters of government. He underestimated the new Kaiser. William was determined to rule as well as to reign, and resolved to dispense with Bismarck as soon as decently possible.

William and Bismarck were soon at odds over foreign policy. William questioned some of the basic assumptions on which

Bismarck's diplomacy was based, especially the need to maintain links with Russia. They also disagreed over social policy. Unlike Bismarck, William was confident that he could win over the working class by a modest extension of the welfare system, including an end to child labour and Sunday working. Bismarck, by contrast, favoured further repression. Thus in 1889 he proposed to make the anti-Socialist law permanent. William was not against renewing the law (he too feared socialism) but he wanted the measure watered down. Bismarck refused. He was then let down by the Reichstag which rejected his entire bill in January 1890. This was a sign that his political power was crumbling. In February 1890, with new Reichstag elections under way, William issued a proclamation promising new social legislation. The absence of Bismarck's counter-signature from this proclamation, which he had bluntly refused to sign, caused a sensation. The election was a disaster for Bismarck. His Conservative and National Liberal allies lost 85 seats while the Radicals gained 46 seats and the Socialists won 24 seats. The 'opposition' was again in control of the Reichstag.

Bismarck was trapped between an Emperor bent on having his own way and a hostile Reichstag. In an attempt to recover his position he proposed an extraordinary scheme: the Reichstag would be asked to agree to a large increase in the army and a new and extremely repressive anti-Socialist law. If, as was probable, they refused, an assembly of German Princes would meet, alter the constitution and drastically curtail the powers of the Reichstag. William refused to support his plan and relations between the two men became even worse.

In March the two quarrelled bitterly about the right of ministers to advise the monarch. Bismarck had revived an old order first issued in 1852 by Frederick William IV, which forbade ministers to approach the King (of Prussia) except through the Minister-President. Bismarck interpreted this to mean that all ministers must obtain permission from him as Chancellor, before they could discuss any government business with the Emperor. William was not prepared for such restrictions and commanded that the 1852 order be immediately withdrawn. At a stormy interview Bismarck nearly threw an inkpot at William and then enraged him by letting him see a letter from Tsar Alexander III very disparaging of his talents. William now sent Bismarck an ultimatum – resign or be dismissed. Three days later Bismarck sent a letter of resignation in which he justified his actions, claiming (wrongly) that the real difference between William and himself lay in the Kaiser's pursuit of an anti-Russian policy. This letter was not made public until after Bismarck's death. The official announcement implied that he had resigned for health reasons and that William had made every effort to persuade him to change his mind. In reality Bismarck retired with ill grace to write his memoirs and innumerable newspaper articles, invariably critical of William. Rumour had it that after his retirement he always placed his money with the reverse side, the German eagle, uppermost, because he could not bear to look at the false face of the Kaiser. Failing to exert any influence on policy, he was even heard to speak in favour of republicanism: kings he said were dangerous if they had real power.

After 1892 Bismarck's health began to fail. He died in July 1898. The mausoleum being built for him and his wife, who had died four years earlier, was not ready and his coffin remained in his house until the following spring. On 1 April 1899 on what would have been his eighty-fourth birthday, Bismarck was buried. On his grave were the words, 'A faithful German servant of Kaiser William I'.

c) How Successful was Bismarck?

Although his body was laid to rest, Bismarck's spirit has continued to haunt German history. Historians have argued over his achievements and his reputation, his motives and his methods. Innumerable books have been written about him. By 1895, five years after his resignation, there were already 650 biographies available. Twenty years later there were 3,500 and the number has gone on increasing ever since.

When it comes to primary evidence the problem is not a lack of material but an excess, much of it conflicting. Bismarck left a wealth of letters, articles, speeches and official reports. There were also his voluminous *Reminiscences*, written long after the events and at a time of great bitterness. They are not entirely reliable, for fact was often embroidered with a little fiction. During his time in office, Bismarck frequently made totally contradictory statements at the same time about the same events. Some historians see this provision of contradictory evidence as symptomatic of Bismarck's perversity of mind, a desire to confuse or mislead friends and enemies alike; to a sense of fun, an echo of his joke-playing days in the 1830s and 1840s; to a lack of settled purpose and the inability to think clearly and coherently in abstract terms; or, more probably, simply as a way of 'reasoning out loud', rehearsing a number of different arguments before reaching a decision. Whatever the reason, it means that Bismarck's own evidence needs to be used with caution. A single letter or speech is not necessarily a true reflection of his policies or intentions at any given time.

It is thus difficult to disentangle with any certainty Bismarck's motives, or to decide how far he planned ahead. He knew as well as anyone that in political life nothing is certain: 'Politics', he said, 'is not in itself an exact and logical science but is the capacity to choose in each fleeting moment of the situation that which is least harmful or most opportune.' He was the supreme opportunist, both before and after 1871. His policies can best be described as flexible. It seems reasonable to assume that he did have general long-term aims: pre-1870 these might include war with Austria and the extension of Prussian power over the other German states; post-1870 he generally wished to maintain peace in Europe and build unity within the German Empire. It also seems reasonable to assume that the timing and the exact means of achieving these aims were left to short-term decisions based on the conditions at the time. *Realpolitik* characterised Bismarck's political career from his earliest days. In 1850 he declared that the only sound foundation for a great state is not idealism but 'state egoism' (national self-interest). Thirty years later, his beliefs had not changed. Defending himself against critics in the Reichstag who accused him of sudden changes of policy he said:

> 1 I have always had one compass only, one lodestar by which I have steered: the welfare of the state ... When I have had time to think I have always acted according to the question, 'What is useful, advantageous and right for my Fatherland and – as long as this was only Prussia
> 5 – for my dynasty, and today for the German nation.

Bismarck had critics in his own time and has had many since. It has been claimed that his strategies and tactics were responsible for Wilhelmine and Nazi Germany. However, most contemporaries viewed, and many historians still view, him as a great statesman who achieved most of his aims, both pre- and post-1871. His admirers point out that no other German exerted so profound an influence on German history in the nineteenth century. Germany did not exist when he became Prussian chief minister in 1862. When he left office in 1890 it was Europe's strongest state. This did not happen by chance. It had much to do with his diplomatic prowess. He manipulated situations even if he did not always create them, and he worked hard and successfully to ensure the outcomes he desired. In so doing he won the trust of few but the respect of virtually everyone he encountered. It is not surprising that the old man of 75 bitterly resented the way in which the young Emperor of 30 seized effective control of his creation. It was unfortunate for both Europe and Germany that after 1890 that creation was in the hands of less skilful men.

Working on Chapter 5

How successful was Bismarck's domestic policy? His admirers claim the following:

- While he committed some blunders, he helped to promote the consolidation and modernisation of Germany.
- The German constitution – his creation – was an inspired compromise, a delicate balance between centralism and federalism and between the forces of conservatism and liberalism.
- In the late nineteenth century conflict between state and Church and between the state and socialism was almost unavoidable. While Bismarck's campaigns against 'enemies of the state' were not successful, they were not total failures. Nor, in the context of the time, were his measures particularly repressive.

- For most of the 1870s he worked closely with the National Liberals, putting their – liberal – programme into place.
- He pioneered state socialism.
- His policies assisted Germany's economic development.
- The fact that he remained in power from 1871 to 1890 is testimony to his political skills.
- He was not a dictator. His powers were far from absolute. While he did not approve of democracy, he did not, and could not, ignore the Reichstag which became a focus of German political life.

What points might his critics make?

Answering structured and essay questions on Chapter 5

Consider the following question:

How successful was Bismarck's foreign policy after 1871?

Bismarck's critics claim:

- He was responsible for France remaining embittered.
- He exaggerated the threat of a Franco-Russian alliance.
- His elaborate alliance system was fragile – little more than a form of crisis-management.
- The Dual Alliance, far from being a means by which Germany could control Austria, eventually dragged her into war in 1914.
- His acquisition of colonies had negative results. German colonial ambitions alienated Britain. The colonies proved to be an expensive financial burden, costing the German taxpayer huge sums of money.
- His style – his frequent use of bluster and blackmail – created a legacy of distrust.
- His influence is often exaggerated. Economic and military strength was the basis of German power – not Bismarck's diplomatic skill. The desire of all the powers to avoid a major war was more important in ensuring peace than Bismarck's diplomacy.

Write an essay answering these charges and making the case for Bismarck.

Source-based questions on Chapter 5

Source A: Dropping the Pilot

DROPPING THE PILOT.

Source B: In an interview soon after his retirement, Bismarck was quoted as saying:

1   I had seen it [my dismissal] coming. The Emperor wished to be his own
    Chancellor, with no one intervening between his ministers and himself
    ... He had ideas which I could not approve. And our characters did not
    harmonise. The old Emperor asked my opinion about everything and
5   told me his own. The young one consulted other people and wished to
    decide for himself. I too wanted to go, though not just at the moment
    when he sent two messengers to hurry me. Matters of importance for
    the Reich were in progress, and I did not wish to see my achievements
    of a quarter of a century scattered like chaff. Yet I'm not angry with him,
10 nor perhaps he with me.

Source C: Wilhelm II, speaking to friends in 1888.

I shall let the old man shuffle on for six months then I shall rule myself.

1. Study Source A.
    What does this source suggest was the main reason for Bismarck's dismissal? (*3 marks*)
2. Study Sources A, B and C.
    How useful and reliable is the evidence presented in Source B? To what extent does it conflict with Sources A and C? (*7 marks*)
3. Study Sources A, B and C.
    Using your knowledge and the three sources explain why Bismarck fell from power in 1890. (*15 marks*)

Further Reading

There are scores of excellent books on nineteenth-century Germany and on Bismarck. It is impossible for most students to consult more than a few of these. However, it is vital that you read some. It is a common complaint of all history examiners that candidates do not read widely enough. The following suggestions are meant to serve as a guide.

1 General Textbooks
Most general histories of nineteenth-century Europe deal with Germany. Among the best are:
J.A.S. Grenville, *Europe Reshaped 1848–1878* (Fontana, 2nd edition, 2000)
M.S. Anderson, *The Ascendancy of Europe 1815–1914* (Longman, 1999)
D. Cooper, J. Laver and **D. Williamson**, *Years of Ambition: European History 1815–1914* (Hodder & Stoughton, 2001)

2 General texts on Germany
The best general history remains:
W. Carr, *A History of Germany 1815–1990* (Edward Arnold, 1991)
The following are also useful:
D. Blackbourn, *The Fontana History of Germany 1780–1918* (Fontana, 1997)
M. Fulbrook, *German History since 1800* (Edward Arnold, 1997)

3 Texts on German Unification
Try and read one of the following:
J. Breuilly, *The Formation of the First German Nation-State 1800–1871* (Macmillan, 1996)
W. Carr, *The Origins of the Wars of German Unification* (Longman, 1991)

4 Texts on Bismarck
Perhaps the best book on Bismarck is:
Edward Crankshaw, *Bismarck* (Macmillan, 1981)
This is not a straightforward narrative and needs a basic knowledge and understanding of Bismarck's life for it to make much sense.
Entertainingly written but not entirely reliable is:
A.J.P. Taylor, *Bismarck: the Man and Statesman* (New English Library, 1974)
A very useful review of Bismarck's life and achievements is:
Bruce Waller, *Bismarck* (Blackwell 1997)

5 Texts on Germany after 1870
The relevant chapters in the following can all be recommended:
S. Lee, *Imperial Germany 1871–1918* (Routledge, 1998)
L. Abrams, *Bismarck and the German Empire 1871–1918* (Routledge, 1995)
D.G. Williamson, *Bismarck and Germany 1862–1890* (Longman, 1997)
W.J. Mommsen, *Imperial Germany 1867–1918* (Edward Arnold, 1995)

Index